WRECKED ON THE CHANNEL ISLANDS

D1312531

WRECKED ON THE CHANNEL ISLANDS

David Couling

STANFORD MARITIME
LONDON

Other books by David Couling

Bournemouth Then and Now
– with John Peters and Michael Ridley

An Isle of Wight Camera 1865–1914

Steam Yachts

Stanford Maritime Limited
Member Company of the George Philip Group
12–14 Long Acre   London WC2E 9LP
Editor Phoebe Mason

First published in Great Britain 1982
Copyright © David Couling 1982
Set in Monophoto Garamond
by Tameside Filmsetting Ltd, Ashton-u-Lyne, Lancs.
Printed in Great Britain by Butler & Tanner Ltd,
Frome and London

British Library Cataloguing in Publication Data
Couling, David
  Wrecked on the Channel Islands.
  1. Shipwrecks—Channel Islands—History
  I. Title
  363.1'23'094234   DA670.C4

ISBN 0-540-07399-7

Acknowledgements

I am deeply grateful for the kindness and hospitality shown to me while working on this book in the Channel Islands and to the many people who have freely supplied information and loaned their precious photographs. For without their help and encouragement it would have become an impossible task.

THE CHANNEL ISLANDS
Mrs B. Allsopp, Guernsey; Mr D.G. Archer, Guernsey; John Babbe, Guernsey; Mrs J. Baber, Guernsey; Mr M. Beckford, Guernsey; Jeff Belshaw, Guernsey; Mrs Coles and the staff of the Candie Museum, Guernsey; Mr D.F. Clark, Guernsey; Mrs Le Comee, Jersey; Victor Coysh, Guernsey; The family of the late J.M. David, Guernsey; Jack Diamond, Guernsey; Grahame Lawson, Alderney; The proprietors of Norfolk Lodge, St Peter Port; Mr H.T. Porter, Jersey; The Editor and staff of the *Guernsey Evening Post;* The Editor and staff of the *Jersey Evening Post;* Miss D.E. Cook, Librarian, Mr B. Hassall and Mr M.J. Hays of the Priaulx Library, St Peter Port; The staff of the RNLI Guernsey station; The staff of the RNLI Jersey station; Eric Sharp, Guernsey; St Peter Port Harbour authorities; the staff of the St Peter Port signal station, White Rock; Mr Henry A.G. Robilliard, Assistant Manager, Sealink UK Ltd, Guernsey; The Chief Officer and officers of the States of Guernsey Police; The Chief Officer and officers of the States of Jersey Police; Mr Carol Toms, Guernsey; Tony Tittering, Jersey Maritime Museum, St Brelade; Dave Trotter, Guernsey; John Upham & Sons, Guernsey; John Wallbridge, Guernsey; Mr and Mrs Ken Wilson, Alderney Museum.

MAINLAND
Ministry of Defence, London; the Royal Air Force Museum, London; Lloyds Register of Shipping; Mr N.F, Stripp, Rescue Records Supervisor, RNLI, Poole; Ms Susan Freeman, Search Dept, Public Records Office, Richmond; Mr E.S. Greenhalf, Trinity House, London; Mr H.A. Breton, Peter Ferrer, Les Kennedy, Mr D. Kingsbury, Mr R. Murley. The masters, officers and crews of the *Earl Godwin* and *Caledonian Princess*, Sealink UK; Mr Shorter, Manager, Sealink UK Ltd, Weymouth. Mr Bunny Trickett, Managing Director, Southern Sea Services Hampshire Ltd, for supplying diving equipment and assistance.

My special thanks are due to Richard Keen of Guernsey for his generosity and friendship to a mainlander, and to Mrs J.M. David for her most generous and valuable assistance. Also to Brian and Wendy Evans, who opened their home giving me the much needed peace and quiet in which to work.

Last, my thanks to Ruth and Carol for bearing with me while I wrote this book.

Abbreviations used in the Text

B & CSP Co.	Brighton & Continental Steam Packet Co. established 1847; taken over by Maples & Morris in 1851. Known as the London, Brighton & South Coast Railway Co. from 1867 until 1923 when it became the Southern Railway Co.
B & SCR Co.	Brighton & South Coast Railway Co. It became the London, Brighton & South Coast Railway Co. in 1867; and in 1923 the Southern Railway Co.
GST Co.	Guernsey Steam Tug Co.
GWR Co.	Great Western Railway Co., established 1854.
JSP Co.	Jersey Steam Packet Co.
L & SWR Co.	London and South Western Railway Co. 1862–1922.
NBSP Co.	North British Steam Packet Co.
PCI & BS Co.	Plymouth, Channel Islands and Brittany Steamship Co.
SESN Co.	South of England Steam Navigation Co., established 1835. Taken over by the South Western Steam Packet Co. 1845.
SS Co. Ltd	Solent Steamship Co. Ltd. Taken over by the London and South Western Railway Co. 1884.
SWSP Co.	South Western Steam Packet Co. 1845. Taken over by the London and South Western Railway Co. 1862.
W & CI SP Co.	Weymouth & Channel Islands Steam Packet Co. Taken over by the Great Western Railway Co. 1889.
MC	Marine casualty; refers to loss not resulting from attack or combat.
HMS	Prefix used before name of warships in Royal Navy and meaning Her (His) Majesty's Ship.
RMS	Royal Mail Steamer. Used to carry cargo and passengers as well as mails.
PS	Paddle steamship.
SS	Steamship.
TSS	Twin-screw steamship.
TrSS	Triple screw steamship.
MV	Motor vessel, i.e. not steam propelled.
TSMV	Twin-screw motor vessel.
TrSMV	Triple screw motor vessel.
USS	Prefix used before name of warships in the US Navy and meaning United States Ship.

Introduction

In this book I have attempted to compile for the first time a collection of photographs depicting vessels that have been either wrecked or severely damaged in the waters around the Channel Islands. Unfortunately, due to storm conditions many vessels in danger could not be photographed until the weather had abated, leaving only the wreckage. However, the written accounts of such losses are more complete, especially those relating to the Bailiwick of Guernsey. The majority of the work carried out in tracing wrecks was undertaken by the late J.M. David whose research into the maritime life of the Islands can only be admired. The researches of Eric Sharp on this subject have also been of great value.

During the early years of photography, illustrations of shipwrecks were rare, no doubt due mainly to the enormously bulky equipment which the photographer had to manhandle over rugged terrain in order to view a stricken vessel. As time passed techniques became more sophisticated and equipment smaller, enabling him to reach a wreck more quickly. By the virtual fact that most shipwrecks take place either offshore or on sparsely inhabited coasts during dense fog or appalling weather, it was seldom that the photographer could be at the scene while the disaster was taking place. Normally, conditions permitting, he would arrive in the aftermath to record the stranded vessel or her wreckage washed up after the preceding storm. With the development of smaller cameras, and then the automobile, it became increasingly easier for the photographer to reach a wrecked vessel before she broke up or disappeared. For the enterprising, the light aircraft eventually afforded the advantage of recording the scene with dramatic effect. A good example of this type of photography may clearly be seen in the illustrations relating to the L & SWR steamer *Princess Ena*, which caught fire in 1935. Later aerial photographs include the *Armas*, *Captain Niko* and *Point Law*.

The reader might remind himself of the position of the Channel Islands in relation to the English and French coasts. They lie to the west of the Cherbourg peninsula and Alderney is nearest to both the mainland of France and to England; its most easterly point is 10 miles from Cape de la Hague, while the northern tip is a little over 60 miles from Weymouth. Jersey is the largest island of the group with an area of 45 square miles; Guernsey covers 24 square miles; and Alderney is $3\frac{1}{2}$ miles long and $1\frac{1}{2}$ miles across. Several smaller satellite islands also come within the group: Sark lies between Guernsey and Jersey, Herm and Jethou are 3 miles east of Guernsey across the Little Russel channel, and Lihou is to the west. Brecqhou is off the west coast of Sark and Burhou is close to the west side of Alderney in a cluster of rocks. Reefs, outcrops of rocks and rocky islets abound, the most notable being the Casquets west of Alderney, the Plateau des Minquiers south of Jersey, and Les Ecrehous midway between Jersey and France. Apart from these dangerous small islands and rock outcrops, the waters are infested with reefs and smaller rocks lying just below the surface of the sea, and these combined with the strong tides make the Channel Islands one of the most hazardous areas for shipping and small craft around the British Isles.

The first known account of a shipwreck describes an event that took place in 1278 when a La Rochelle vessel came to grief on the Castle Rocks, Guernsey. Unfortunately no other facts were recorded, and before 1278 there appear to be no written accounts relating to shipwrecks although it is highly probable that they took place. Indeed, within the last few years evidence has been recovered from the sea bed by local divers which suggests that a Roman vessel may have foundered there during the first century. Two complete amphorae were recovered plus several shards. It is by no means clear whether a Roman vessel actually went down at the site of the finds, however, for it is quite possible that cargo, including amphorae, broke loose from the deck during a storm while the vessel survived.

Within the Bailiwick of Guernsey, which includes the islands of Sark, Herm and Jethou, around five hundred vessels are known to have either sunk or broken up after sustaining major damage. For the Bailiwick of Jersey the figures are considerably less: it should be remembered that Jersey is away from the main shipping lanes and this would account for the smaller number of ships lost. Shipping losses around Guernsey are greatly increased by the inclusion within the Bailiwick of Alderney and the Casquets, which lie near the main shipping lanes. In both areas, however, figures stated for vessels in distress, or which have subsequently sunk, cannot be taken as complete. Undoubtedly many went down with total loss of life without anyone being aware of the tragedy at the time. One such wreck was found in August 1912 when fishermen reported sighting the top of a funnel and a mast covered in seaweed just under the surface near Le Hanois, Guernsey. On investigation it was found that only a quantity of ironwork remained of the mystery ship; the funnel turned out to be her boiler. From the growth of seaweed and barnacles on the ironwork it was concluded that the vessel had been lying on the seabed for less than a year, probably 6 to 8 months. Positive identification of the ship was never achieved, but one point is certainly clear – that those on board perished in sight of land and safety.

Research into the causes of shipping losses around the Channel Islands points to three main factors. One has already been mentioned: the Islands' proximity to the main shipping lanes. There is also the notoriously bad weather coupled with fog, strong tidal streams and underwater rocks. Indeed it is doubtful whether there are many rocks left unscathed by some passing vessel. Finally, human error in navigation must play an important part in the loss of vessels in these waters. As one captain of a Sealink ferry told me, 'You never know. With the volume of shipping in the lanes becoming more congested every day, and the supertankers taking so long before they can stop, you have to be on watch every minute of the day and night. When in Island waters you have to be on your guard even more nowadays: there are so many small boats and yachts about, and there are rocks everywhere – it's as if they almost pop up overnight.' On many occasions ferries owned by the railway companies have come to the aid of stricken vessels in and around these waters, and without their prompt assistance the list of those lost would be far longer. It must be hard for the holidaymaker to imagine, while sitting on a sunny beach gazing out at a distant ship cutting her way through the sparkling sea, that such a scene can quickly turn into a raging inferno. While at sea myself I had the unnerving experience of being in a Force 12, described as a hurricane on the Beaufort scale, while going through the Bay of Biscay. It is a situation which calls for the highest quality of seamanship and one can only admire men who battle with the sea in such terrible conditions.

Conditions must have been very similar for Admiral Balchen in 1774 while in command of HMS *Victory*, approaching the Casquets. She was the fourth of five warships to bear that illustrious name, the most famous being the fifth and last, under the command of Admiral Lord Nelson. Admiral Balchen's *Victory* was a 100 gun first-rater and in her day was recognised as the finest ship afloat of her type. While homeward bound from the Mediterranean with the British fleet she became separated from the body on the night of 5 October, in one of the worst storms the Channel Islands had experienced for many years. At 2 a.m. the keepers of the Casquets lighthouse heard gunfire from the stricken vessel but due to the storm they were unable to give assistance. During the following days wreckage was washed ashore at Alderney which included spars, gun carriages and gilded carvings. Of the 1,100 officers and men aboard the *Victory* not a soul survived that terrible night, making it one of the worst maritime disasters ever to take place in the Channel Island waters.

In the last year of the nineteenth century the foundering of the L & SWR ferry *Stella* can justly be called the *Titanic* of the Channel Islands. Although the loss of life was fortunately less than from *Victory*, the sinking of the *Stella* stunned the Islanders. On 30 March 1899 she struck the Black Rock on the Casquets with the loss of 105 lives. Her master, Captain Riggs, ordered women and children away first in the ship's boats; those left on board had to survive as best they could. The steamer *Lynx* rescued 46 passengers and a further 64 were saved by the *Vera*. *Stella*'s gallant master died with his ship as did stewardess Mrs Mary Rogers who gave up her place in a lifeboat for a passenger, remained on board and perished. One of the more gruesome aspects of the sinking were the advertisements in local newspapers offering rewards for the recovery of drowned relatives.

To Fishermen and Others.

NOTICE.

£25 Reward will be paid to any person or persons recovering the body of the late Mr R.R.L. Rosoman, of Southampton, lost in the *Stella* disaster.

Description: Height about 5′ 4″. Grey beard, mole on right cheek, age 72, dressed in blue cloth, underlinen marked R. Rosoman.

Signed: H.F. *Rosoman*, Post Office, St Peter-in-the-Wood, Guernsey.

Notice to Fishermen and Others. Wreck SS *Stella*. Reward to be given for recovery of bodies as below. Instructions having been left with me, P. Ahier, Avoué [Solicitor], 36 Pollet.

FEMALES

Annie Nisbet, wife of George, Hayter Road, Brixton, fair, age about 37.

E. Nisbet, wife of Frank, Wood Green.

MALES:

R.A. Stewart, Solicitor age 43, of 49 St Charles Square, Notting Hill, London.

Phillip Howard Davis, Gentleman age 48, hair dark, of Angel House, East Hill, Wandsworth. Initials of names will be found on body linen.

Walter Packer, of Deacon's Firm, Walbrook City, height 5′ 5″, light moustache, blue eyes, dressed in blue serge, gold watch and chain and spectacles, name on inside pocket of coat and trousers.

E.W. Murray, age 22, dark complexion, no beard or moustache, initials on underlinen. Relation of Miss Head, 23 George Street, Guernsey.

Report forwith, Private Enquiry Department, Ahier, 36 Pollet, Guernsey. April 1st, 1899.

Disasters at sea do not always involve countless people losing their lives. In 1918 one man was to die in terrible circumstances. On 19 December 1918 the *Iris* was discovered aground east of Fort le Marchant, Guernsey. No one was found on board, but later a body was recovered from Fontenelle Bay and identified as that of the mate. There the story should end, for a man drowned at sea is sad enough, but it took an even more horrific turn. A month later the ketch's owner, R.F. Manning, was found on one of the Humps north of Herm. It appeared that the poor man had managed to reach the islet from his sinking ketch, and had made a rough hut out of the ship's gratings and seaweed. Weak from starvation and exposure, he had been unable to call or signal for assistance from passing boats and had died alone and unknown.

The case of 3,000 ton French steamer *Briseis* caused a headache for the local authorities, and no doubt a different sort for many of the islanders of Guernsey. When the *Briseis* struck the reef off Vazon Bay, Guernsey in October 1937 she was carrying over 7,000 casks of wine. Looting was rife, and many people were found drunk on the beach. There were strange tales of a mystery ship standing by the *Briseis* at night, and of boatmen being hurriedly called from the Gaumont Cinema and being rushed to the bay by the police to give chase to the mystery looters. Today one may still see the *Briseis* by diving on her and with luck come up with some wine still good enough to consume.

However, diving on her or the countless other wrecks in these waters should not be attempted by the untrained or inexperienced. Over the last few years several visiting divers have lost their lives, and even the most experienced should be on guard against the strong and treacherous tides and currents which occur, and the ocean swell. The majority of wrecks around the Channel Islands are owned by someone, in many cases by divers who may have spent many years searching for a particular ship. They will not take kindly to outsiders descending on their territory and removing items from their ship. By far the best way is to get in touch with the local diving club, which will advise you on particular wreck sites to dive on.

But one is by no means restricted to viewing the sunken remains of the great vessels. In Guernsey there is the excellent Fort Grey Maritime Museum for those who are interested in the sea and her dangers. Among the many displays are five cases showing items recovered from local wrecks which include HMS *Splitley*, lost in 1777, *Boreas* 1801, SS *Yorouba* 1888, SS *Brisies* 1937 and MV *Prosperity* 1974. Today, with many sophisticated navigation and radio aids there is less danger of ships striking, but as cargo vessels get larger and larger, and especially in the case of chemical carriers and oil tankers. a new danger arises, that of pollution. If the giant ore carrier *Elwood Mead* which stranded off Guernsey in 1974 had been carrying oil and had ruptured her tanks, then the consequences to marine life, sea birds and the coastline would have been catastrophic. Let us hope that this situation never arises in the Channel Islands.

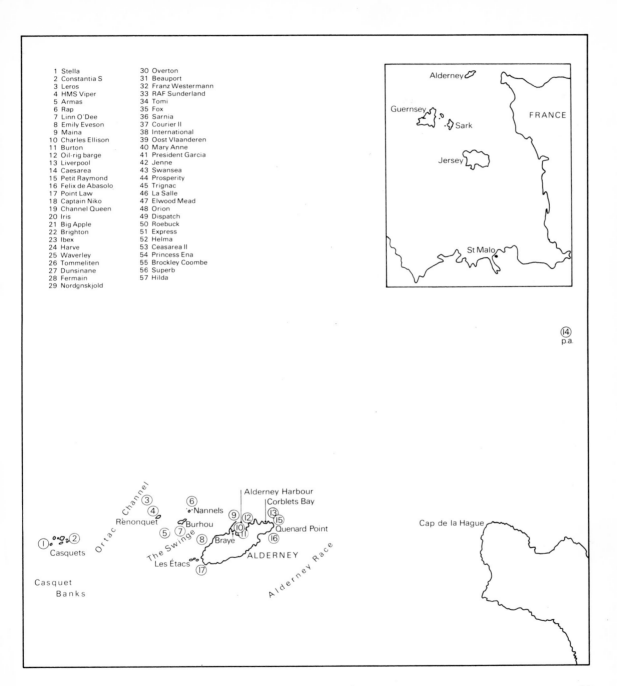

1 Stella
2 Constantia S
3 Leros
4 HMS Viper
5 Armas
6 Rap
7 Linn O'Dee
8 Emily Eveson
9 Maina
10 Charles Ellison
11 Burton
12 Oil-rig barge
13 Liverpool
14 Caesarea
15 Petit Raymond
16 Felix de Abasolo
17 Point Law
18 Captain Niko
19 Channel Queen
20 Iris
21 Big Apple
22 Brighton
23 Ibex
24 Harve
25 Waverley
26 Tommeliten
27 Dunsinane
28 Fermain
29 Nordgnskjold

30 Overton
31 Beauport
32 Franz Westermann
33 RAF Sunderland
34 Tomi
35 Fox
36 Sarnia
37 Courier II
38 International
39 Oost Vlaanderen
40 Mary Anne
41 President Garcia
42 Jenne
43 Swansea
44 Prosperity
45 Trignac
46 La Salle
47 Elwood Mead
48 Orion
49 Dispatch
50 Roebuck
51 Express
52 Helma
53 Ceasarea II
54 Princess Ena
55 Brockley Coombe
56 Superb
57 Hilda

Alderney

Guernsey

Sark

FRANCE

Jersey

St Malo

⑭
p.a.

Ortac Channel

Rènonquet

③
④
⑥ Nannels
⑨ ⑫
⑬
⑮
Burhou
⑤ ⑦
⑩
⑪
Alderney Harbour
Corblets Bay
Quenard Point

① ·°·◦◦ ②
Casquets

⑧ Braye
⑯
The Swinge
Les Étacs
⑰
ALDERNEY

Cap de la Hague

Casquet
Banks

Alderney Race

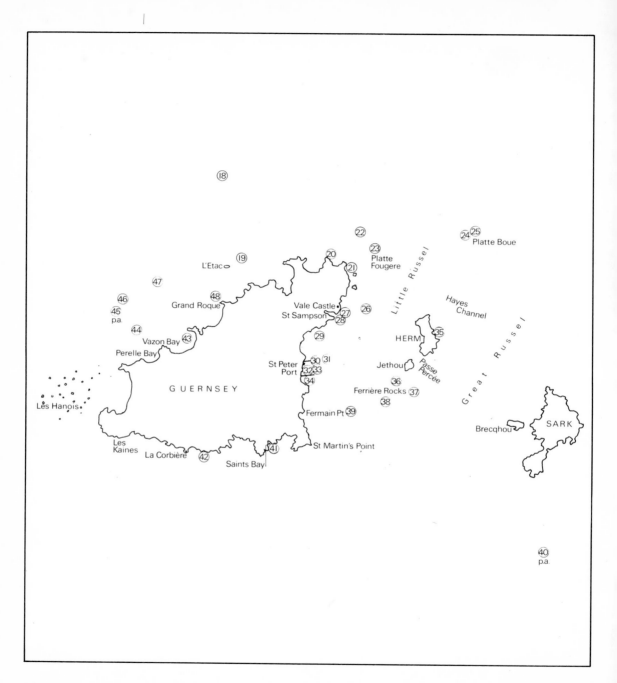

Les Hanois

L'Etac ○

Grand Roque

Vazon Bay

Perelle Bay

GUERNSEY

Les Kaines

La Corbière

Saints Bay

St Martin's Point

Fermain Pt

St Peter Port

St Sampson

Vale Castle

Platte Fougere

Platte Boue

Little Russel

Hayes Channel

HERM

Jethou

Passe Percée

Ferrière Rocks

Great Russel

Brecqhou

SARK

⑱

⑲

⑳

㉑

㉒

㉓

㉔ ㉕

㉖

㉗

㉘

㉙

㉚ ㉛

㉜ ㉝

㉞

㉟

㊱

㊲

㊳

㊴
p.a.

㊵
p.a.

㊶

㊷

㊸

㊹

㊺
p.a.

㊻

㊼

㊽

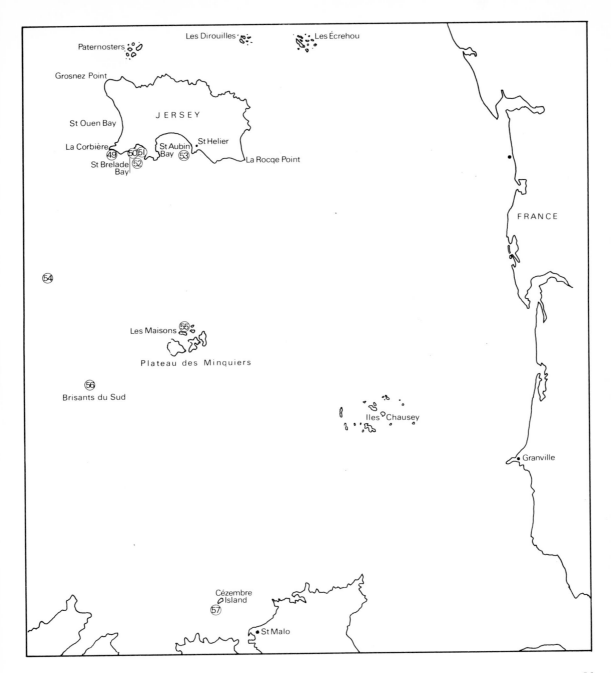

Paternosters

Les Dirouilles

Les Écrehou

Grosnez Point

J E R S E Y

St Ouen Bay

La Corbière

St Aubin Bay

St Helier

49 50 51 52 53

St Brelade Bay

La Rocqe Point

F R A N C E

54

Les Maisons 55

Plateau des Minquiers

56

Brisants du Sud

Iles Chausey

Granville

Cézembre Island

57

St Malo

Les Casquets

The name 'Casquets' is derived from the French 'cascade' which aptly describes the outcrop of rocks near Alderney with the over-falls and vicious races which perpetually flow around them. Over many years the Casquets have been the scene of countless disasters. About 1722, the owners of the ships passing certain dangerous rocks called the 'Casketts', off Alderney, applied to Thomas Le Cocq, the Proprietor of the rocks, to build a lighthouse and offered him ½d per ton when their vessels passed the light. Le Cocq obtained a patent in 1723 and Trinity House decided that a light of particular character to distinguish it from those on the shores of England and France was needed. Three separate lights in the form of a horizontal triangle were proposed, and three towers containing closed fires – coal fires burning in glazed lanterns – were erected. These lights, called St Peter, St Thomas and Dungeon, were first exhibited on 30 October 1724. The lease granted to Le Cocq by Trinity House lasted for 61 years at a rent of £50 per annum.

The three Casquet lights reverted to Trinity House in 1785, and were later converted to metal reflectors and Argand oil lamps; a revolving apparatus was fitted to each tower at the Casquets in 1818, and the three towers were raised by 30 feet in 1854.

The original towers at the Casquets still stand today and are in constant use. The main navigational light is the highest, 120 feet above sea level, flashes five times every 30 seconds, and can be seen for 17 miles in clear weather. The east tower contains the diaphone fog signal which gives two blasts every 60 seconds. The third tower contains radio beacon equipment.

An extraordinary wartime incident occurred on the Casquets on 2 September 1943. While the lighthouse was manned by seven German Keepers it was raided by the British; offering no resistance, the keepers were taken to England for interrogation, no doubt thankful to be off the rock. Why the raid ever took place is somewhat of a mystery, but it is thought to have been a training exercise.

The Guernsey signal station, at St Peter Port. Calls are received from shipping requiring pilots, tugs or wishing to enter the harbour. Here too Mayday calls are picked up from ships in distress and relayed to the appropriate emergency services.

Orion

ABOVE

Nan Halfweeg, flown back from Japan to lead Wijsmuller's salvage team on the island. He had directed the successful salvage of the *Elwood Mead* off Guernsey in 1974.

ABOVE

Orion was a jack-up rig, mounted piggy-back on the ocean-going barge *Federal 400–2* for the tow to Brazil. The rig's insured value was around $16,950,000 most of which was secured on the London market. Although the rig itself suffered very little damage, the barge's bottom was badly holed by the rocks, and further damaged by the weight of the rig as it worked in the heavy seas.

LEFT

The lifeboat taking salvors off the barge under the rig. Working against the clock and the weather to refloat on 10 February, they had left getting off too late and were trapped on board. A helicopter was unable to lift them off because of the bad conditions.

At 8.25 p.m. on 1 February 1978, the Guernsey Police Headquarters received a telephone message from the watch house at St Peter Port that the giant oil rig *Orion* had broken loose from her tug in heavy weather and was drifting free some 20 miles north and west of the island. The jack-up rig, owned by the International Drilling Co. of the USA, was 250 feet high and displaced 19,000 tons, and at the time was under tow from Rotterdam to Brazil with a crew of thirty-three. The island emergency services were immediately alerted and the St Peter Port lifeboat went out to aid those on board. The tug *Seefalke* struck bottom twice in her last desperate attempt to reconnect the tow, damaging her bottom so that only continuous pumping kept her afloat. The rig was driving towards the shore fast and the lifeboat moved in: two men were taken off, though the crew were reluctant to leave.

Lit up like a large building, *Orion* ran

Divers had to work in the exhausting pull of the waves to inspect the barge's hull and blast away rock outcrops that were piercing and holding it.
Groningen, 4,200 hp, one of the enormously powerful deep sea Wijsmuller tugs which, with the tugs *Typhoon,* 14,000 hp, and *Schotland,* eventually pulled the *Orion* off.

aground on the Grandes Rocques 150 yards from the beach at 11.25 p.m. By midnight two Royal Navy Sea King helicopters from Culdrose in Cornwall had lifted off all but six of the remaining rig crew. During this operation the wind was gusting between 60 and 70 knots, and when the tide swung the rig the helicopters were in even greater danger and had to abandon operations. Two more men were taken off by breeches buoy, and the last four by 'copter the next day.

The Dutch salvage firm Bureau Wijsmuller monitored the situation by radio in Ijmuiden and sent two tugs to the scene. After several days they were awarded the salvage contract, and on 27 February were finally able to refloat the rig and tow it away to Cherbourg.

Richard Keen

ABOVE

The successful refloating of the *Orion* on 27 February was watched by hundreds. It was probably the last chance to get the rig off, for a storm was moving in from the Atlantic, the barge underneath had tilted and was in bad shape, and the rig had been cut free and was resting precariously on top of it. At high water the tugs pulled the rig off the barge's deck by brute force.

LEFT

Groningen, 4,200 hp, one of the enormously powerful deep sea Wijsmuller tugs which, with the tugs *Typhoon*, 14,100 hp, and *Schotland*, eventually pulled the *Orion* off.

One of the leading salvage experts on Guernsey is Richard Keen. Over last fourteen years he has dived and worked on most of the wrecks around the island. Because of his expert knowledge of tides and dangerous currents, Richard was commissioned by the Dutch salvage company Wijsmuller, to carry out the underwater surveys of both the super-freighter *Elwood Mead* which ran aground off Vazon Bay, in December 1973, and the giant oil-rig *Orion*, blown ashore by gale force winds near Grandes Rocques in February 1978. Richard's interest in Channel Islands shipping has lead him to become a recognised authority on shipwrecks in the area; he is also active in the field of nautical archaeology and hopes one day to open his own wreck museum.

Tomi

The fishing vessel *Tomi* was driven ashore below the south wall of St Peter Port, on the night of 11 July 1977. Her crew of five Germans made shore safely but *Tomi*, which had recently cost her owners £15,000 to convert to a motorized sailing vessel, fared worse, being declared a total loss. She was later bought by Mr Ted Foster, who managed to salve her.

Big Apple

Tuesday, 14 June 1977 brought near-disaster for the 44 foot racing sloop *Big Apple*. Built at a cost of £85,000 to race in the Admiral's Cup series at Cowes, she hit a rock and sank when approaching Beaucette Marina, Guernsey. Her crew made shore safely and organized salvage operations immediately, but it was not until two days later that *Big Apple* was raised and taken into St Peter Port. The damage consisted of denting and several tears in her aluminium hull and damage to interior woodwork.

The yacht was shipped out on the deck of the *Norman Commander* to Portsmouth on 22 June, and then on to Joyce Bros. of Southampton for repair: she later returned to racing.

RIGHT
The crew salvaging some of the yacht's gear and their personal effects from the grounded hull.

BELOW
Flotation bags attached to the hull by divers, which enabled *Big Apple* to be lifted at high water and then towed into the harbour.

Described at the time as 'the most out-and-out of
racing machines', the Irish contender for the Admiral's
Cup after being lifted out of the harbour. It was to cost
thousands of pounds to put her back in racing
condition.

Oil-rig Barge

An unusual casualty of the sea occurred on the morning of 25 November 1974, when a 300 foot American-owned oil-rig barge broke her tow-line and was carried by the currents onto the rocks at Bibette Head, Alderney. She was worth in the region of one million pounds, and being towed from Stavanger in Norway to Jacksonville, Florida.

During the following days the barge was towed from Bibette Head to Braye Harbour where she was eventually salvaged. The captain of the motor vessel *Gulf Fleet 8*, which was towing the barge when it broke away, presented the States of Alderney with a case of scotch, for the help he received from the island.

The photo shows the barge about to be taken under tow again.

Point Law

Point Law, a 1,500 ton Shell-Mex BP tanker which supplied fuel oil to the Channel Islands, came to grief when she ran ashore at the southwest end of Alderney in the early morning of 15 July 1975. Her crew of twelve were all rescued safely, but the vessel's life ended quickly in the pounding of the storm-tossed seas. The wreck was later sold for scrap to salvage expert Richard Keen.

OPPOSITE PAGE
A dramatic view from the cliff while one of the crew of the *Point Law* is rescued from the air and the lifeboat stands by.

BELOW
The tanker has broken into three sections here, because of the stresses on her hull. She was eventually cut up for scrap.

LEFT
The Captain and crew of the *Pegase* arriving at St Peter Port on board the lifeboat.

BELOW
Fire burning in the *Pegase*. The empty lifeboat on the starborad side was lowered by the crew, but they later transferred to the Guernsey lifeboat.

Pegase

This 10,000 ton Swiss owned and Panamanian registered freighter became a loss by fire on 15 February 1975. Of the crew of twenty-seven, one died in the blaze while the others were rescued by the St Peter Port lifeboat. *Pegase* was later towed to Falmouth for damage assessment.

The after half of the *Prosperity*, breaking up further in the same gale that caused her loss.

M.V. Prosperity

On 16 January 1974 the St Peter Port Harbour Master was informed by the Signal Station at White Rock, Guernsey that a cargo vessel by the name of *Prosperity* required assistance. This telephone call became the curtain raiser to one of the worst disasters to take place around the shores of Guernsey during the 1970s. By the time the grim episode had reached its end eighteen lives, including a young woman, would be lost by drowning. The position of the doomed vessel was given as 20 to 25 miles west of Les Hanois lighthouse at 16.50, and with this information the St Peter Port lifeboat *Sir William Arnold* put to sea. At 21.00 coxwain John Petit reported that the violence of the storm, then Force 11 to 12, made it impossible to see anything, due to the excessive spray and twenty-five foot waves and the bad light, and his lifeboat was recalled.

John Petit and his courageous crew made a second attempt to find the *Prosperity* the following day, leaving port at 06.30. They searched along the south coast of the island until directed toward La Conchee Rock, where they sighted the ship hard aground. She had been lost with all hands, in sight of the giant *Elwood Mead*, a victim of the same bad weather. During the next few hours the lifeboat picked up seven male bodies from the sea a mile or so off Pleimont and transferred from a German steamer a further four bodies found in the sea. In all sixteen dead were recovered, though the bodies of the master, Captain Geoggiou Kastellorizias, and the boatswain Uzoglan Ibrahim, were never recovered.

It was later discovered by the authorities that the *Prosperity*, 2,085 tons, was owned by the Bahi Shipping Co. of Piraeus, Greece and registered at Famagusta. The ship had left Pateniemi in Finland on or about 7 January, sailing via the Kiel Canal and North Sea to the Mediterranean. Her cargo was in excess of 3,800,000 cubic metres of timber.

Due to the violent storm the ship quickly broke her back, releasing her cargo into the foaming seas which threw it onto the rocky shores of Guernsey. There is no doubt that a great deal of wood was collected by the islanders for their own use, which necessitated the local police guarding the washed-up cargo. But it should be added in their defence that a statement had been put out that '. . . people may now take timber from the beach up to twelve midday.' This, of course, caused a surge of activity along the shore, but the statement was

The burial of the six Pakistani seamen, with full Muslim rites, at Le Foulon Cemetery, 23 January 1974.

Part of the cargo of timber washed ashore.

found to be incorrect and much of the missing timber was returned.

The Guernsey Police, who acted beyond the call of duty during the disaster, had the unenviable task of dealing with the dead, consisting of five Greeks, six Pakistanis, a Turk, an Algerian, an Indian and two negroes. They arranged for the bodies of the Greeks to be flown home, and the others were buried on the island at Le Foulan, on the 23rd and 29th of January. The dreadful loss of life moved Mr Jack Diamond, of The Missions to Seamen Society, to raise a fund for a permanent memorial to the lost crew of the *Prosperity*. Through his efforts and those of other islanders, a memorial was erected at L'Eree.

LEFT
The ship's bow section has moved away from the rest of the hull and can be seen at the right of the picture.
BELOW
The end of the *Prosperity*. All that remains of her today is part of her engine, which may be seen at low tide.

Elwood Mead

The huge ore carrier *Elwood Mead* became an extra Christmas attraction on Guernsey when she ran aground off Vason Bay on Christmas morning in 1973. Owned by United International Bulk Carriers and Hendy Co. of Los Angeles, she had left Port Dampier, Australia on 22 November 1973 on her maiden voyage for Rotterdam and Dunkirk, laden with 122,954 long tons of lump iron ore. Her detour from safer water in the English Channel was mainly caused by bad weather conditions and errors in navigation, which resulted in her being stranded for 61 days.

The ship was eventually pulled free by the

BELOW

These pictures were taken in good weather: much of the time it was bad, slowing salvage work and threatening to break up the ship.

The early attempts to get the *Elwood Mead* off before the weather deteriorated relied on lightening by pumping out and pressurized air buoyancy, but failed. The hull was impaled on rock pinnacles, and aground over most of its length. The ore cargo had to be pumped overboard, the hull patched and sealed, and anchors laid out ahead and to the side. The hull was then raised by pumping and blowing out water, and pulled off with three tugs and the ground tackle.

RIGHT

The salvage operations were assisted by the Royal Navy, who helped ferry out vital salvage machinery.

Wijsmuller salvage company on a 'no cure, no pay' contract, and one can only admire the salvage crew for their tenacity, working in generally bad weather. Even after towing to the Hook of Holland, bad weather and the sheer size of the vessel made discharging her cargo to enter drydock very difficult. The cost to her owners and insurers is not fully known, but there is no doubt that it was astronomical.

The damage she had sustained was published by Lloyds of London: 'on the starboard side of the hull, the flat bottom plating is ruptured from the stern coffin plate to the bulbous bow. At frame 30 the damage sweeps up to the side shell plating, reaching a height of 22 feet at frame 70 and continuing along the length of the flat of the side at heights varying from 8 to 16 feet. On the port side the damage is less severe, some plating on the flat bottom between frames 200 and 230 appearing intact. The rupturing on the side shell is confined below the 3 foot mark.' After costing £13m to build, *Elwood Mead* was sold for £8¼m to the Good Faith Shipping Co. who eventually had her refitted in 115 days. She was later renamed *Good Leader* and resumed a useful career at sea.

Part of the crushed and torn hull plating, seen in drydock. The bottom was damaged along most of its length.

Armas

On 26 November 1973 the Cypriot cargo vessel *Armas*, 2,545 tons, struck the Renonquet reef in poor weather near Burhou, a small island off Alderney. Her crew were rescued by two helicopters from the British naval ship *Engadine* which was luckily close at hand, although one of the crew of twenty-three was lost.

Armas, bound for Le Harve in ballast, was firmly wedged on rocks. During the following months she was incessantly pounded by the heavy winter seas and by the summer of 1974 very little of the wreck was left, as the second photograph shows.

President Garcia

A large ship surprised a courting couple who were parked in their car at the fishermen's harbour at Saints Bay, Guernsey as she ploughed through the bay and came to rest a few feet away. The *President Garcia*, bound for Rotterdam from Manilla with 9,500 tons of copra, presented a fantastic sight to the hundreds of people who came to see her. She had run in at high water thus missing many of the rocks in the bay and, incredibly, had avoided hitting any of the small craft moored there, possibly more by good luck than seamanship.

By a combination of removing cargo, plugging holes and cracks, pumping and finally tugs, the ship was pulled off a week later on 20 July 1967 and anchored off St Peter Port, before being towed stern first to Rotterdam for repairs.

Captain Niko

In May 1973 the *Captain Niko* succumbed to the battering of heavy seas and sank three miles off Rousse. The Dutch freighter, carrying 9,100 tons of fertilizer, ran into rough seas 18 miles west of Les Hanois: taking on water, she began to list to the extent that she became unmanageable. The supply ship tender *Turbot* came to her aid, taking her in tow in an attempt to get her into calm water off the northern tip of Guernsey. While under tow *Niko*'s list developed to 52° and became increasingly worse; with less than 4½ miles to safe water the tug had to release her tow line. Within eight minutes *Captain Niko* rolled over and sank in 144 feet of water. An eighteen year old seaman died when the crew abandoned ship; the others were all saved.

The photo shows her shortly before she sank.

Constantia S

The Casquets claimed yet another ship in the January gales of 1967 when the unladen British oil tanker *Constantia S* went aground on the eastern end of the rocks. The Guernsey lifeboat *Euphrosyne Kendal* arrived at the scene to aid the endangered crew, and also on hand were the Trinity House tender *Burhou* and the British Rail passenger steamer *Sarnia*. *Burhou* picked up sixteen crew, *Sarnia* a further ten from a lifecraft, and the ship's captain was lifted off the rocks by a French helicopter which later transferred him to Guernsey. *Constantia S*, 8,686 tons gross, eventually broke in two and became a total loss.

La Salle

On 28 May 1965 the Monrovian steamer *La Salle* struck Les Grunes rocks off the west coast of Guernsey. The ship remained stuck hard and fast for some time until eventually she broke her back and sank. The crew were all safely taken off by the St Peter Port lifeboat.

The photograph shows the ship's back broken in two places, just forward of the accommodation and bridge, and farther aft where her side plating is buckling.

RAF Sunderland

One of the most unusual wrecks to take place in the Bailiwick of Guernsey occurred in 1954, when a RAF Sunderland flying boat struck a submerged rock while landing outside St Peter Port. Her crew managed to manoeuvre their crippled aircraft into the harbour, though it was later found that the damage was beyond repair, causing her to be scrapped. The photo shows her after being towed to the careening hard in the harbour, where she dried out at low water.

MV Brockley Coombe

The *Brockley Coombe* of Bristol, under the command of Captain F. Saint, struck Les Minquiers reef in poor visibility and soon afterward broke up and sank on 15 December 1953. Her crew of eleven were saved by the St Helier lifeboat *Elisabeth Rippon*. The coxwain was accorded the thanks of the RNLI inscribed on vellum, for the rescue of the crew.

SS Fermain

29 December 1952 saw the loss of the 1,086 ton steamer *Fermain*, owned by O. Dorey & Sons of Guernsey. Carrying coal to St Samson's Harbour, Jersey, *Fermain* had reduced steam in order to enter, but due to a delay she was caught in strong winds and tide. Unable to raise steam in time, she drifted onto the Black Rock outside the harbour. Because coal was an essential fuel for the island a causeway was constructed from the coast road to the vessel and her cargo was removed into waiting lorries by cutting a hole in the side of the hull. *Fermain* was later sold to John Upham & Sons of Guernsey who broke her up for scrap.

TOP LEFT
A causeway has been built up to the stranded ship and a hole cut in her side to enable workmen to remove the cargo of coal to waiting lorries.

ABOVE LEFT
As the level went down, lorries could be driven right inside the *Fermain* to load coal.

TOP RIGHT
The funnel being cut away at high water.

ABOVE
The funnel, taken ashore as the ship was cut up for scrap.

Oost Vlaanderen

The 421 ton armed motor vessel *Oost Vlaanderen* was bombed and sunk by Allied aircraft on 23 May 1943 a mile and a half off St Peter Port. Today she lies 80 feet down on the sea bed, on an even keel with her guns pointing forwards as though waiting for the next air attack. While making a dive on her, she struck me as a most melancholy sight: one half-hoped *Vlaanderen*'s telegraph would ring 'full ahead' and with her engines throbbing she would steam away from her watery grave.

The ship in happier days, on the Danube before the war.

Franz Westermann

VP 205 *Franz Westermann*, a 481 ton auxiliary patrol vessel, was sunk by Allied aircraft on 15 June 1944 after an attack on the St Peter Port area. The rare wartime photograph shows the partly submerged wreck, and was taken at great risk to the photographer.

Helma

The motor schooner *Helma* was one of many marine casualties of Allied attacks during the occupation of the Channel Islands during the Second World War. On 15 May 1943 Allied planes flew around the south and west coasts of Jersey, attacking a German patrol boat and sinking it off St Brelade Bay. During the attack *Helma* was badly hit. Records do not give her fate, but it is possible that she was too severely damaged to carry on her duties at sea.

The *Helma* after being attacked by Allied fighters. It will be noted that the quality of the photograph is poor: it was taken by an islander at great risk to himself, for being found in possession of a camera and film incurred the severest penalty from the German authorities. One can only admire the unknown photographer for his brave act in recording the scene.

SS Arnold Maersk

While delivering a cargo of over 200 thousand-pound bombs to the German occupying forces on Jersey, the 1,966 ton *Arnold Maersk* became a casualty, foundering on the Grunes aux Dardes rocks off Jersey on 22 May 1943. Some years later her deadly cargo was successfully blown up by a Royal Navy bomb disposal team.

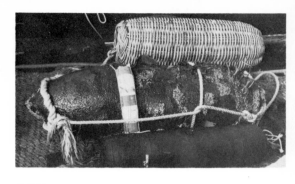

The end of a 1000 lb bomb, detonated by the Royal Navy. The explosions were heard clearly in Jersey and the inhabitants were warned to leave their windows open to avoid glass being broken by the blast.

ABOVE
One of the 1000 lb German bombs waiting to be lowered back into the sea after being fitted with a plastic explosive charge.

Henny Frickle

The boiler and triple-expansion engines are all that are left of the *Henny Frickle*, 300 tons, lost through accident in Braye Harbour, Alderney in 1943. A German deep sea steam trawler, she was built at Lubeck in 1924. At the outbreak of war in 1939 she was taken over by the German Navy and given the wartime designation PB 703. At very low tide it is stilll possible to see her remains.

SS Tommeliten

Registered in Belgium, *Tommeliten*, 228 tons, struck the Platte beacon off Bordeaux, Guernsey on 6 February 1938. She was bound from Port Talbot to St Sampson, Guernsey with a cargo of coal and was a regular trader to the Islands. After striking, her crew of twelve landed safely. The *Tommeliten* was later refloated and taken to St Sampson's Harbour, where she was salved.

SS Overton

This three-masted Liverpool steamer struck a submerged object in St Peter Port and sank on 25 February 1933. She was soon raised and her damaged hull repaired.

SS Beauport

The *Beauport*, 920 tons deadweight and 190 feet long, was originally named *Sunniside* and built in 1920 by the Forth Ship Building Co.; in 1926 the Sea Transport Co. purchased her as a coal-carrier. She was wrecked on the Agenor Rocks near St Peter Port on 16 February 1930; her crew, under Captain Christian, were all rescued. The following June she was pulled off the rocks and towed a short distance before being anchored. Five days later she was again taken in tow and moored on a sandy bottom near the White Rock. At this point the salvage operations went sadly wrong with *Beauport* settling in 10 feet of soft sand. Several attempt were made to free the steamer by using suction pipes, but without success. In September she was finally blown up and sections of her hull were taken out and sunk off Havelet Bay. An Action of Damages taken out by the Board of Administrations against the Sea Transport Co. for a £6,250 salvage claim in 1931 resulted in the company going into liquidation in 1935.

LEFT
The salvage vessel *Bullger* using suction pumps on the virtually submerged *Beauport* in June 1930.

BELOW
The wreck listing heavily after settling farther into the soft sandy bottom. Not long after this salvage attempts were abandoned.

Early morning in St Helier harbour during the late 1930s. The two steamers in the background are, from left, the Southern Railway Co. vessel *Isle of Jersey*, built 1930, and the *Lorina*, constructed for the L & SWR Co. in 1918.

SS Ribbledale

The *Ribbledale* left London on 23 December 1926 bound for Jersey. Arriving at Bouley Bay on the 27th after a very rough passage, she anchored outside Ronez to await orders to enter port. During the early part of the evening a strong gale blew up causing the steamer to drag her anchor. Although her master ordered 'full ahead' she drifted broadside onto the rocks and became a total loss.

Her anchor chains can be seen in this photograph, taken the next day, and the anchor light on the forestay.

Iris

The last hours of the ketch *Iris*, wrecked on 19 December 1918. She had gone aground 400 yards east of Fort La Marchant, Guernsey. At low tide the wrecked vessel was boarded but no one was found. Within a few days a man's body was washed ashore at Fontenelle Bay, and later found to be the mate of the *Iris*. A month later a second body was found on Galeaux, one of the islets of the Humps, north of Herm. At an inquest, it was found that he, a Mr R.F. Manning, had made a hut out of seaweed and the vessel's grating: but had died of starvation and exposure. Apparently the poor man had survived for some time within the sight of help from passing ships.

TSS Princess Ena

The *Princess Ena* was built in the record time of four months by Gourlay Bros of Dundee for the L & SWR Co. and launched on 25 May 1906. At the time she was the largest steamer owned by the company, 1,198 tons gross and 250 feet overall. Her main route was between Southampton and St Malo, also calling at Jersey on excursion trips and at times carrying the mail from Jersey. The ship's career was full of incident and finally her end came with a disastrous fire at sea.

On 20 May 1908 while on route to St Malo *Princess Ena* struck the Paternoster Rocks off Jersey. While there was no immediate danger, the lifeboats were lowered away with passengers. However, the vessel floated off and the passengers returned. The ship arrived at St Helier next day with six feet of water in her forward hold. Having landed her passengers, she made temporary repairs and then left for Southampton to have extensive repairs carried out.

In August 1923 the steamer once again came to grief, this time on the Minquiers; at 5.45 a.m. on the 13th she struck the rocks in dense fog. As a precaution two of her lifeboats were lowered with fifty passengers, but at 7 a.m. she managed to float clear of the rocks and begin to proceed to St Malo. Unfortunately, due to the fog which was still in the area, the two boats which had been launched could not be found; an hour and a half later they were picked up by the Southern Railway Co. steamer *Bertha* which had earlier answered the *Princess Ena*'s SOS call. The passengers eventually arrived at St Malo none the worse for their ordeal.

Princess Ena's destruction began on 3 August 1935. Arriving at Jersey at 10.40 on Saturday

morning, her passengers – five hundred Boy Scouts, Cubs, and members of the Boys Brigade – disembarked for their annual holiday. Sailing from Jersey at midday for St Malo with only officers and crew on board, the steamer caught fire when approximately nine miles off La Corbière. All fought courageously to get the fire under control, but within a very short time it had taken hold and a large part of the ship was engulfed in flames. The decision having been made to abandon ship, the crew first dropped her anchors to reduce the danger to other shipping in the area. The crew of forty-two were picked up by the States tug *Duke of Normandy* and the French steamer *St Brieuc*, both having raced to the scene of the disaster after picking up a distress call radioed from the *Princess Ena*.

During the rest of the day and into the night, the fire took its remorseless hold on the ship and by early morning it could be seen that she was in her death throes. By mid-morning her stern had started to settle and at 1.26 p.m. the sea began to rise over her and pour in through the portholes, until at last her stern disappeared. Clouds of belching smoke engulfed her forward end and with a swirl of smoke and steam the bows sunk beneath the waves.

Captain Lewis and the officers of the *Princess Ena* had stayed with their doomed ship through the long night and into Sunday morning on board the Southern Railway Co. steamer *Ringwood*. As the final moment came and she began to slip beneath the sea Captain Lewis, his officers and the crew of the *Ringwood* bared their heads and the *Ringwood*'s ensign was lowered in a last salute to a gallant ship.

Tr SS Ceasarea II

Ceasarea II and her sister ship *Sarnia* were the first turbine powered ships on the Channel Islands run. They were owned by the L & SWR Co. and both could carry 980 passengers; *Caesarea II*, 1,505 tons gross, was built in 1910 by Cammell Laird at Birkenhead. (Caesarea is the Latin name for Jersey, and Sarnia for Guernsey.)

Leaving Jersey just after 7.15 a.m. on 7 July 1923 under Captain Smith with 373 passengers on board, the ship made her way slowly out of St Helier: conditions were bad as there was fog in the area. When near Noirmont Point she began to make way for the incoming steamer *Alberta* and in doing so struck the Lignornet

Rock. Captain Smith, realising his ship was taking water fast, turned back to St Helier giving four short whistle blasts to inform other ships of the urgency of the situation. *Caesarea*'s lifeboats lowered away as were the *Alberta*'s, which was standing by; all the passengers were quickly tranferred to the *Alberta* without any loss of life and very little panic. Taking water fast, *Caesarea* headed for the safety of St Helier and again came to grief, striking the Oyster Rocks. Her stern was not deep in the water and she was stuck fast, and with the approach of high water she was almost covered.

Salvage divers went down to inspect her hull, finding that she had lost one propeller and had several gashes in her side. By 20 June salvage operations had been successful and the ship was slowly towed by the tug *Canute* to the mainland for repair. Later in the year *Caesarea* was sold to the Isle of Man Steam Packet Co. and renamed *Manx Maid*, to be eventually resold in 1950 and scrapped.

Fifty-one years later in 1974, a reminder of the *Caesarea*'s accident was recovered from the seabed by a team of Royal Navy divers led by Tony Titerington, Jersey's leading expert on wrecks and diving: he and a local police diver, PC Derek Horsall, located her bronze propeller near Noirmont. With the aid of a tug the giant propeller was lifted from the reef, and although eroded with time it was still in good condition. The propeller was eventually placed on display at Elizabeth Castle, Jersey as a monument to the *Caesarea II*.

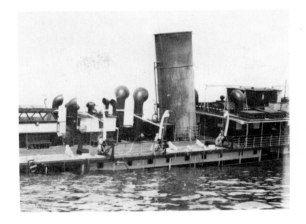

OPPOSITE ABOVE
The launching of *Caesarea II* at Cammell & Laird in Birkenhead on 26 May 1910. She cost £75,000 to build.

OPPOSITE BELOW
Excursion passengers at Weymouth before sailing for the Channel Islands, around 1920.

TOP RIGHT
The half-submerged promenade deck, looking forward.

The arrival of the Southampton mail boat at St Helier.

SS Emily Eveson

The *Emily Eveson*, 630 tons, bound from Swansea to Rouen, ran onto the beach in Clonque Bay at midnight on 19 May 1922 and became a total loss. Her crew took to the boats and their cries for help were answered by the barking of the dog at Clonque Cottage. The occupants of the cottage raised the alarm and guided the crew to the safety on the Alderney shore.

Jenne

The French ketch *Jenne* of Treguier, 86 tons, was bound from Spain to Dunkirk when at 11.30 p.m. she struck the rocks between La Bigard and Corbiere on 27 March 1913.

On finding that the vessel could not be refloated, she was broken up and her masts, deck and cabin fittings salved. Her hull was sold for £5 to a Mr Martel, who owned the salvage steamer *Pioneer*, and the cargo of 40 tons of ore for £1.

Mary Anne

This 280 ton brigantine from Fowey was off the west coast of Guernsey on 27 May 1917 when she was attacked by a German submarine patrolling in the area. After firing on the *Mary Anne* a boarding party placed explosives on board and detonated them. Although the blast caused severe damage it did not in fact sink the vessel. In the meantime her crew were allowed to leave unharmed in the boats, making shore later in the day. Several days later the *Mary Anne* was found drifting on her side south of Sark by the *Courier*, which towed her into St Peter Port (where she is shown here). In 1919 she was bought by W.G. Hubet & Co. for £1,250 and was later converted into an auxiliary schooner.

SS Rhenania

The Dutch steamer *Rhenania*, 1,600 tons, went ashore on the Noir Houmet at La Lague, Burhou at 5 a.m. on Sunday, 7 April 1912. She had been carrying general cargo and cattle to Spain. Many of the cattle were drowned when the forehold filled with 10 feet of water after the impact. The crew were compelled to stay on board because of looting by the islanders and in time her cargo was salvaged. The ship later became a total wreck.

Charles Ellison

The Rochester, Kent sailing barge *Charles Ellison*, loaded with stone from Braye Harbour, broke her moorings and drifted onto the rocks behind the Alderney breakwater. Her crew were saved but the barge became a total wreck.

The accident happened on 7 January 1911 only five days after the loss of the *Burton*, seen in the background.

SS Burton

The *Burton* had left Braye Harbour on 7 January 1911 after having loaded stone during the day. Shortly afterwards she hit the Grois Reef, damaging her hull badly. Flares were lit and seen by the crew of the steam tug *Courier*, which went out to her. As nothing could be done in the poor light, it was not until early morning that *Courier* began to tow the *Burton* back to Braye. In the meantime her crew had taken to the ship's lifeboat and landed safely in the harbour. The vessel was beached in Braye, but in the heavy pounding of the seas she broke her back and became a total loss.

oks of "Charles Ellison" and "Burton"

TSS Roebuck

The *Roebuck* and her sister ship *Reindeer* joined the Great Western Railway Co.'s Channel Island service in July 1897. *Roebuck* 1,281 tons gross, 280 feet long, was built by the Naval Construction and Armament Co. at Barrow. Her career was packed with incident and included two fires, one major wrecking, and eventually sinking after ramming a battleship at Scapa Flow.

The first incident took place at Milford Haven on 26 January 1905: fire was discovered in the saloon and quickly spread to the galley and through the ship. Due to the amount of water pumped into her by the fire tenders, *Roebuck* eventually keeled over and sank. In hindsight,

Roebuck at low water on Les Kaines, seemingly inextricably stuck.

this probably saved the ship from total destruction. At the same time she was worth around £30,000 and it was deemed worthwhile to have her salved. It was later found that the fire had been caused by faulty asbestos lagging on the stove pipe in the saloon. In October 1908 fire once again broke out, this time in her engine when halfway between Guernsey and Weymouth. The captain ordered the fire hoses to be manned and the passengers to go forward of the blaze. The fire was put out in twenty minutes after causing extensive damage to the deck paint, woodwork and interior panelling.

Roebuck's main claim to fame occurred in July 1911 when she became one of the most visually dramatic wrecks to take place in the Channel Islands. Leaving St Helier at 8.30 on 19 July 1911 she encountered fog almost immediately. Off Noirmont Point the fog lifted slightly, giving those on board a sight of the rocks. However, as she approached the western end of St Brelade Bay *Roebuck* suddenly crashed into Les Kaines rocks. The passengers, over a hundred, took to the boats and landed at Les Creux pier in St Brelade Bay. The States tug *Duke of Normandy* went out with the Harbour Master and retrieved all their belongings, while the pilot cutter stood by. As the tide began to ebb the result of *Roebuck*'s accident could clearly be seen; she was wedged between the two outermost rocks of the Kaines, her bows rising up off the rocks and her stern practically submerged. After two weeks of intensive salvage work she was pulled clear and beached in St Brelade Bay, watched by enthusiastic trippers on board the *Courier*. *Roebuck*'s damage included a 40 to 50 foot gash in the port bilge, a large hole aft, and another on the starboard side. After being patched up she left for Southampton in August for major repairs. At a subsequent enquiry *Roebuck*'s master, Captain Le Feuvre, was found to be at fault by the vessel

being set in towards the coast by some abnormal tide or current, which he had not allowed for: his certificate was suspended for three months.

In 1914 *Roebuck* was taken over by the Admiralty for war service and renamed HMS *Roedean*. While in Scapa Flow on 13 January 1915 she broke away from her moorings in high winds and hit the battleship *L'Imperieuse*. In the collision *Roedean*'s bows were stove in and she sank shortly afterwards in 30 feet of water. No attempt was made to salvage her.

SS Felix de Abasolo

During the early morning of 7 June 1910 the
Spanish steamer *Felix de Abasolo*, 2,076 tons,
under the command of Captain Sturrino,
stranded on Les Boufresses reef in thick fog.
The Bilbao steamer, bound from Newcastle
with coal and general cargo for Genoa,
encountered thick fog when making down the
Channel. At 2.30 a.m. they sighted the lights of
Cape de la Hague and headed northwest;
shortly afterwards they struck the reef. Soldiers
from Fort Albert on Alderney rescued the
crew, landing them on Raz Island from where
they were later taken to Alderney. Like so
many vessels stranding around the Islands, she
broke her back and became a total loss.

Maina

The stranded yacht is on the breakwater rocks at Alderney in June 1910. She was later refloated without any damage to her hull.

In the background and just to the right of *Main*'s foremast can be seen the stemer *Terra*, 4,500 tons, which hit the Grois Ledge in the same month.

SS Rap

In June 1910 three steamers came to grief around the shores of Alderney: *Felix de Abasolo* on 7 June, *Terra* on 11 June, and the *Rap* on 18 June. In each case the stranding was due to heavy fog.

Rap, 1,416 tons, had run onto the Pierres du Butes reef near Burhou. Her mixed crew of English, Swedish, Norwegian, Russian, Finnish and American seamen were towed in their lifeboats by the launch *Lita* to the safety of Braye Harbour without any loss of life. The *Rap*, bound for Gibraltar laden with 1,700 tons of coal, broke her back and then broke in two, as can be seen in the photo. In four days she had been almost completely smashed to pieces.

SS Linn O'Dee

The *Linn O'Dee*, 282 tons, a regular trader to the Islands and at the time bound from Portsmouth to Guernsey in ballast, was wrecked when she struck on the southwest end of Burhou on 18 June 1910. As she passed down the Swinge in heavy fog at 11 p.m. her foghorn could be clearly heard by the inhabitants of St Annes on Alderney. Shortly afterwards she grounded on a submerged ledge known as La Lague. Her crew took to the boats with no idea where they were, due to the adverse conditions, and they spent an uncomfortable eight hours before eventually landing at Corblets Bay near Chateau a l'Etoc, Alderney. From there they were taken to Guernsey by the *Courier* where they were looked after by the Shipwrecked Mariners Society. The *Linn O'Dee*, built at Glasgow in 1883, was later declared a total wreck.

Nordgnskjold

On 28 February 1910 the Russian brigantine *Nordgnskjold* ran onto the rocks at Spur Point, Guernsey and became a total wreck. The 319 ton vessel had left La Rochelle in France eleven days earlier bound for Llanelly in Wales and loaded with pit props. She encountered heavy weather at sea and part of her canvas was carried away when she was west of Guernsey.

On the afternoon before she was wrecked *Nordgnskjold* was near St Martin's Point when she was hailed by the tug *Alert* to ask if she needed assistance. The captain declined but took a pilot on board, a Mr G. Legg, who took the brigantine to the southernmost end of the Channel where she dropped anchor, and he returned to St Peter Port. At 7 a.m. the next morning the vessel's cables parted, and at the mercy of the currents and without sail up *Nordgnskjold* drifted onto Spur Point, striking at 8.15 a.m.

For the first night after grounding the crew remained on board, but the next day they left as her hull was badly torn making her unstable. The crew stayed on Spur Point, for some time living in the cabin of the wrecked *Ella*, which had come onto the rocks on 11 January 1887.

Nordgnskjold was later bought by a Mr J. Martel, who broke her up.

The coal quay in St Peter Port around 1910.

QUEEN VICTORIA & PRINCE ALBERT
LANDED XXIV AUGUST.
MDCCCXLVI.

International

While carrying 330 tons of anthracite coal from Swansea, this brigantine struck the Musee Rock and then drifted onto the Ferrieres rocks on 23 January 1908. Apparently, after passing St Martin's Point on Guernsey she was caught in the grip of strong currents running towards the Ferrieres. The crew let go the anchor to stop the vessel's drift, but this had little affect and she became wedged on the rocks. The damage to the hull caused the water to pour in and there was very little the crew could do but abandon ship; they landed safely at Albert Pier having had enough time to collect their effects. The ship became a total loss.

The wreck of the *International*. The island in the background is Herm.

SS Leros

The German steamer *Leros* 7,500 tons, struck the Frette Rock near Burhou on 29 May 1906. Fishermen from Alderney went out to her to rescue the crew but were turned away at the point of a gun and told to keep off. The intrepid fishermen decided that discretion was the better part of valour, immediately withdrew and began to row back to the island. But as they were returning, they heard an explosion and saw the Germans making for the lifeboats, only to find that the plugs were out and they began to take in water. Hearing cries for help, the fishermen returned and picked up the crew.

The next day much of the cargo of sewing machines were removed to the beach, and quickly 'acquired' by the islanders. No doubt the following winter months saw an increase in dressmaking in many of the cottages on Alderney.

Leros was later found to be a total loss, apart from her engines, and her hull was blown up.

SS Swansea

The *Swansea*, carrying 1,300 tons of coal and bound from Swansea to St Malo, struck near the Grune Rocks northwest of Guernsey on 23 July 1906. Her crew of fourteen men and a boy were under the command of Captain Hall from Jersey. They encountered dense fog almost immediately after leaving port and did not sight land until after their vessel had foundered. After hitting, *Swansea* managed to slip back into deep water where the crew took to their boats as hull damage was considerable and she was taking in water fast. With the arrival of the steam tug *Assistance* the sinking steamer was taken in tow and beached in Vazon Bay. In the following days *Swansea*'s cargo of coal was quickly dumped over the side to lighten the vessel and temporary repairs were carried out. Hundreds of sight-seers were attracted to Vazon Bay, and enterprising photographers, F.W. Guerin and Messrs Banks, each produced a set of postcards showing the wreck scene. The ship was later salved.

RIGHT
Salvors working in Vazon Bay, at high water.

The stranded *Swansea* at Vazon Bay after being towed off the rocks by the tug *Assistance*.

RMS Courier II

The first *Courier* was owned by the Alderney Steam Packet Co. and sailed between Guernsey and Alderney and to Cherbourg, from 1876 until 1913 when she became redundant. *Courier II* entered service at St Peter Port in July 1883; she was slightly larger (151 tons gross, 130 feet long) than her predecessor and used by the Alderney & French Trading Co. in the same capacity. Among all the craft that worked the Channel she was the best known and loved. During her career she was instrumental in helping to rescue many ships and seamen in distress including the brig *Odin*, steamer *B. Remenery*, brigantine *Natch*, ketch *Pearl*, a French open barge steamer *Ville de Maloga*, the bark *Tytty*, SS *Burton* and the schooner *Bess Mitchell*.

Courier II had several mishaps, the worst taking place in 1906. After leaving Creux harbour on Sark at 5 p.m. to return to St Peter Port she struck the Annons rocks south of Jethou in fine weather and sank shortly after, at 5.30 p.m. Of thirty-nine passengers and crew

ten were drowned. While there was no panic, the accident happened so quickly that only one lifeboat managed to get away, filled with women. The rest of the crew and passengers were left struggling in the sea. Fortunately the steam tug *Alert* quickly arrived on the scene and rescued those who were still clinging to wreckage.

During the following months salvage work was carried out to refloat *Courier II* and on 31 July she arrived at St Peter Port, slung between two barges and towed by the tug *Assistance*. One sad event occurred on 5 August as *Courier II* was being brought farther into the harbour. Members of the crew, including the mate, a Mr Masterton, and Seaman Denning, while on board the wreck in the evening decided to see if any of their belongings were still inside. On making a search with the aid of

Her masts gone, the weed-grown wreck is pumped out in St Peter Port.

candles they found the body of a middle-aged man with a lifebelt around his waist in the ladies' cabin. The police were called and the body was later identified as a Mr Lang. One can only surmise that the unfortunate man had been trapped below deck as the ship went down; his wife had been saved at the time of the disaster. At the Court of Enquiry Captain Whales was found guilty of negligence, in that he should have been extra careful as the vessel was sluggish and slow in answering the helm, and in getting too close to the Gouliniere Rock.

On 5 October 1906 *Courier II* was towed back to her builders, Day & Summers at Southampton, for major repairs. By December she had returned to the Islands and resumed normal service. The rest of her days were relatively quiet, serving in the First World War in camouflage grey and occasionally being escorted by French seaplanes based at St Peter Port while on trips to Guernsey to Alderney. In the Second World War she found herself on Admiralty service on the Clyde. The gallant little steamer returned to her home waters in July 1947 amid much cheering and blowing of foghorns. Sadly, before the year was out she had been sold, her owners finding her too old and expensive to operate; she was broken up for scrap in Holland in 1950.

The ship was then beached where repairs and cleaning up could be done at low water, watched by spectators.

HMS Viper

The 344 ton *Viper* was the first turbine driven destroyer constructed for the Royal Navy, launched in 1899. She was the direct development from *Turbinia*, the earliest turbine driven steam yacht, built by Charles Parsons in 1897. *Viper*'s turbines produced 10,000 h.p. to achieve a speed of 32 knots; in fact she easily ran at this speed, her maximum being 37 knots. During her short career (1899–1901) she was rated as the fastest ship in the Navy.

On 3 August 1901 *Viper* under the command of Lieutenant Speke was taking part in manoeuvres off the Casquets. In the afternoon the visibility had deteriorated due to fog and her speed was reduced from 22 knots to 16 knots. On sighting Torpedo Boat 81, an 'enemy' ship, *Viper* raised her speed back to 22 knots in order not to be seen by the other craft. While making this maneouvre she struck the Renonquet reef off Burhou. The impact ripped out her bottom, making her a total loss (the terrific damage can be seen in the photo).

Viper was eventually blown up and sold for scrap, her armament being salvaged by the Navy. At a Court of Inquiry, Lieutenant Speke was reprimanded for careless action; it was indeed fortunate that there was no loss of life.

It is interesting to note that *Viper*'s sister ship HMS *Cobra* sank five weeks later near Flambrough Head, with a heavy loss of life.

Petit Raymond

This Nantes schooner, bound for Southampton from Le Légué, St Brieuc with a cargo of potatoes, ran ashore at Belle Bay near Houmet, Flourens on 19 September 1906. Heavy winds had split her mainsail when she was in the Channel and she was forced back towards the Guernsey coast.

The *Guernsey Weekly Press* gave an interesting account of the scene.

The *Petit Raymond*, swept forward by the immense incoming rollers, grounded on a sandy bottom. This was at low tide. The Coastguards, under the direction of Chief Officer Barber, were soon on the spot. Coastguard man Phillip Phillips volunteered to swim out, at great personal risk, taking a lifeline. This was attached to the vessel's boat and the five crew with their effects were pulled safely ashore. Shortly afterwards, the captain ordered his men to pull him back. They then returned to the shore. In the meantime the tide was rising and the spectators knew that the vessel would sooner or later ground on the jagged rocks which skirt the top of the bay. Although called upon by his crew and the people ashore to come on land, the captain refused. Roller after roller struck the vessel, and she at last came to rest on the needle-sharp rock known as Little Bonnie. The keel soon ground itself away and the vessel was seen to be near complete sinking. Several seagoing men at last got the boat launched again, a rope was paid out and again the vessel was reached. The captain once more refused to leave so he was forcibly lifted over the side and deposited in the boat. This was just in time: two minutes later the ship lurched over and was completely swamped.

On suspecting that there might be pilfering, the authorities ordered a detachment of guards from the Manchester regiment to keep watch on the ship night and day. The photo was taken not long after the ship came ashore, for her canvas and hull do not show the battering she was to receive: eventually she became a total wreck.

SS Trignac

The *Trignac* went aground at La Soufleurese, a reef off Perelle Bay, Guernsey on 27 July 1905. Her main claim to fame was the distress caused by her cargo of rotting maize: the stench hung over the island for over a week while her cargo was being unloaded. The ship was later salved.

The *Trignac* taking on cargo at St Peter Port. In the background can be seen Castle Cornet.

SS Hilda

The 235 foot *Hilda*, 849 tons gross, was constructed in Glasgow for the L & SWR Co. and made her first run to the Channel Islands in 1883. Although she did not founder in those waters, her loss is be included here as she was a frequent visitor to the Islands.

During a blizzard on 18 November 1905 *Hilda* struck the Roche du Jardin rock off the Isle of Cézembre near St Malo in Brittany. The resulting loss of life stunned both the French and the Channel Islanders: 104 passengers and all but one of the crew of 25 including her captain perished in the icy water. Because she stranded on rocks it was almost impossible to lower any lifeboats and one eye-witness reported seeing people crowding around the mainmast and rigging only to be washed overboard by the force of the sea. At a later Inquiry no blame was attributed to Captain Gregory or the crew of the *Hilda*; the loss was ascribed to adverse weather.

SAINT-MALO
Le " Hilda " avant le Naufrage du 19 Novembre 1905   G. F.

SAINT-MALO
The " Hilda " before the wreck
of the 19th November 1905

Saint-Malo --- Naufrage du " HILDA " (19 novembre 1905)
L'arrière du navire et le pont brisé

TOP LEFT
Captain Grégory on the *Hilda*.

ABOVE
The amidships section after the ship had broken her
back.

Saint-Malo -- Naufrage du " HILDA " (Nuit du 18 au 19 novembre 1905)
Scaphandriers recherchant les cadavres

Saint-Cast — Naufrage du " HILDA "
(19 novembre 1905)
La vieille église où furent
déposés les 60 cadavres

OPPOSITE ABOVE
Wreckage washed up on shore.

OPPOSITE LEFT
Divers looking for bodies in the wreck.

TOP
The bows of the ship broke away and were completely
destroyed: pieces of her steel plating can be seen on the
rocks.

ABOVE
Six of the French survivors. Between eighty and ninety
of the *Hilda*'s passengers were French onion-sellers
returning to Brittany from England.

LEFT
The church at St-Cast where sixty dead were taken.

Dunsinane

The barque *Dunsinane*, 130 feet long and drawing 14½ feet, was built at Dundee in 1847. While under the command of Captain P. Mahy and carrying general cargo she was wrecked on the Black Rock on 13 August 1904. The ship had taken on 500 tons of granite at St Sampson's Harbour and sailed at 7 p.m. for London. As she cleared the breakwater she encountered a strong tide running to the north and started drifting; the wind had fallen making her helpless. With the tide running fast she drifted towards Vale Castle and struck Black Rock. On board were the captain's wife and child, who were landed on Guernsey at Bordeaux.

During the next few days the cargo was removed by taking out planking from her hull and loading the stone onto waiting carts on the beach. Later the wrecked barque was sold to a Mr Macpherson of South Shields for £13 and broken up.

ABOVE
The ship attracted many spectators, who are here watching her cargo of stone being unloaded.

RIGHT
The immense weight of the hull, cargo and spars has pressed in the side of the ship. Some of the granite blocks which she carried can also be seen here.

Liverpool

The *Liverpool* has the dubious distinction of being the largest sailing ship wrecked in the Channel Islands. The British four-master was three days out from Antwerp bound for San Francisco with general cargo when she stranded on the northeast end of Alderney on 25 February 1902. Thick fog had engulfed the waters around the island during the early part of that morning. The *Courier* had managed to negotiate the Swinge, blowing her whistle every few seconds, and getting away for Cherbourg at 11.30 a.m.; her crew later thought it strange that they had not heard the *Liverpool* sounding her foghorn, or even caught a glimpse of the great ship as they had passed within a short distance of her. By noon the fog had lifted sufficiently for the islanders to stare in amazement in the direction of Corblets Bay at what they at first thought was a huge house rising above the hill, actually the four massive masts of the *Liverpool* with all their square sails set, giving the optical illusion of a great white-washed building. According to her master, Captain Lewis, at midnight they had been 16 or 18 miles off Barfleur, the wind being ESE and very light. They lost sight of the Barfleur light at 1 a.m. because of fog, and were then on a westerly course. At 3.30 they began to take soundings which they continued at 6 a.m. with a sounding of 40 fathoms. At 8 a.m. the sounding was 36 fathoms, and course was altered to WNW at the same time. The 10 a.m. sounding was 35 fathoms. At noon breakers were sighted ahead but *Liverpool*'s helm refused to answer and she was driven ashore, striking about 12 miles SSE of her assumed position. At the inquiry Captain Lewis was found at error in his handling of the situation in that 'damage was not caused by a wrongful act or in default of the master, but he failed in not sufficiently taking into account the dangerous incurrent'.

Liverpool became a great attraction for the islanders of both Alderney and Guernsey, with

excursions to view the scene. Pilfering was done from French boats in the area and by the islanders, which necessitated a guard on the ship and salvage operations taking place as soon as possible. Many of the crew of thirty-seven complained that they had been robbed of their personal possessions, which they had left on board the *Liverpool* after they had abandoned her.

The wreck was bought by a consortium of

five persons for the sum of £250 with the intention of selling off the ship and the cargo in lots. Among the cargo were: wines and spirits – 1,000 cases and 400 casks, including brandy, wines, cognac, whiskies, gin, liquers, clarets, sherries, ales, etc; groceries – 6,000 cases of soap, mineral and an assortment of waters, vinegar, mustard, vegetables, sardines, salad oil, olive oil, curry powder, preserves; and 160 bags of sulphur. The sale on 26 May consisted of 3,000 marble slabs, 500 marble table tops, 200 tons of square, flat and round iron and steel, wrought iron, quicksilver bottles, 300 cases of glass, rope, canvas and ship's sirens. The ship and her remaining cargo were sold on 27 and 28 May including boats, two complete sets of sails and one new spare set, anchors, chains, donkey boiler winches, 250/300 tons of iron and steel, etc. By the end of the day the sale had fetched well over £8,000.

ABOVE
Excursion passengers leaving the 'Little Courier' at Braye Harbour, around 1900.

TOP RIGHT
A busy scene at White Rock, St Peter Port, around 1900. The departure of the mail boat for the mainland was accompanied by a brass band (centre); the Royal Mail wagon has transferred its mail to the ship and can be seen by the goods shed (right).

RIGHT
The G & W R Co. shop *Roebuck* leaving St Peter Port amidst farewells and bound for Southampton, c. 1900.

TSS Ibex

The *Ibex*, 1,161 tons gross and 265 feet long, was built in 1891 by Lairds and suffered two incidents at sea during her career, in 1897 and 1900. At that time it was not uncommon for steamers on the Channel Island route to race each other, both to prove which was the fastest ship on the crossing, or to reach port first to catch the tide. At St Helier large ships had difficulty in berthing except at high water as the rise and fall could be more than 30 feet. Also, that port had no really deep channels to allow the larger ships entry, so if a mail ship missed high water at St Helier she had to moor outside in the roads. This would cause considerable inconvenience to the passengers, they and the mails having to be conveyed in small boats to the harbour.

On Good Friday, 16 April 1897, the L & S W R Co. steamer *Fredrica* left Southampton for Guernsey and Jersey over an hour late due to the boat train being delayed. Farther down the coast at Weymouth, *Ibex* experienced the same situation, sailing fifty minutes late for the Channel Islands. At 7.32 a.m. *Ibex* docked at Guernsey, disembarking her passengers and some of her cargo; *Fredrica* arrived fifteen minutes later. By 8.05 *Ibex* began to make her way towards St Helier, and at 8.15 *Fredrica* followed. Both ships had now to race at top speed to catch the high tide at St Helier before it began to ebb at 9.45 Within an hour *Fredrica*, the slightly faster ship, had come up beside

Ibex as they approached St Helier. Captain Le Feuvre of the *Ibex*, noting that time was running out, decided to take the Noirmontaise Channel and turning to port steamed toward the *Fredrica*. Although there was just room enough for the ships to pass each other. Le Feuvre changed his mind and turned towards deep water to go outside the Noirmontaise Channel again. This manoeuvre proved fatal and *Ibex* ended up on the rocks of the Noirmontaise, while *Fredrica* carried on unscathed. The amount of damage sustained by the ship was considerable: seven propeller blades were smashed and two compartments were flooded from a 13 foot tear in her hull. The crippled steamer eventually made for Portelet Bay where the 160 passengers were taken ashore by her

OPPOSITE PAGE
Ibex aground at Portelet Bay in April 1897, after striking the rocks at Noirmontaise.

BELOW
Cleaning up after six months underwater in the Little Russel channel.

boats and those of the *Fredrica* which was standing by. By Sunday temporary repairs had been carried out to the *Ibex* and she was towed to St Helier, going later to Barrow for permanent repairs. Her captain was found to have been careless in navigation and his certificate was suspended for six months.

On 5 January, 1900 *Ibex* was approaching Guernsey in clear weather when she struck a rock off Platte Fougere and sank with the loss of two lives. Her master stated that he was proceeding to St Peter Port at half speed with the sea calm and the weather clear, when nearing the Brays they struck a submerged rock, which took him by surprise. Giving orders to head for Herm to beach the ship, they had proceeded for only twenty minutes before she sank in the middle of the Little Russel, the passengers and crew taking to the boats. At the time it was thought that all thirty-five passengers were saved, but divers later found the body of a naval rating in the saloon; it was surmised that the unfortunate man had slept through most of the incident, only waking when the saloon had been engulfed in water and then finding himself trapped. One of the crew also lost his life: he was last seen clinging to the flagstaff. Although his shipmates held out oars from their lifeboats for him to grab, the poor man declined, apparently because he was very timid. It had been impossible to get close to him as the swell was so dangerous that it might have capsized the boats.

The wreck of the *Ibex*, which at high tide was completely submerged, was raised six months later at the cost of £15,000 on a 'no cure, no pay' basis by the Northern Salvage Co. of Hamburg. The steamer later returned to the Channel Islands after being refitted. The total cost of salvage, towing, refitting etc was around £42,000.

The *Ibex* at low water in St Sampson's where she was beached after being raised.

TSS Stella

The worst shipping disaster to take place around the Channel Islands during the late ninteenth century was the loss of the L & SWR Co. steamer *Stella*, sunk with the loss of 105 lives after striking the Black Rock on the Casquets reef in dense fog, on 30 March 1899. The ship, 1,059 tons gross and 253 feet long, had only been built in 1890, by J. & G. Thompson of Clydebank.

An eye-witness account of her last voyage was given by a passenger, Mr James Parton of London.

We left Southampton at 11.15 a.m. and passed the Needles at 12.30. The weather was fine and clear till 2.45 p.m. when we ran into hazy weather. This increased in desntiy, but at no time could we see less than half a mile ahead. Our foghorn was sounded at regular intervals, and the captain was in his place on the bridge from the commencement of the fog. At about 3.45 a great mass of rock, apparently a hundred or more feet high, suddenly loomed up on our port side, abreast of us. At this moment the ship's head was bought around to starboard but it was too late. We were apparently hemmed in by the cruel rocks and after grazing one the *Stella* careered over onto a submerged one before she could be stopped. It was then evident that serious results must follow. The officers without a trace of excitement assured the passengers that if they would remain calm and collected all would be well. The boats were lowered and although only about twelve minutes elapsed before the foundering, four were loaded and got away; the other boats were being prepared for launching. The stewards busied themselves giving out lifebelts and I saw hardly anybody without a belt. The coolness and resource of the officers was ably seconded by the passengers generally. There was no panic or wild rushing for the boats, the blanched faces and the partings between husband and wife alone showing that all realised the peril. I got my wife into the second boat that left, and my own escape in the last boat that got

Captain Reeks, who was lost with the *Stella*.

99

Stella circa 1895, entering St Peter Port.

First Office Hodges, Captain Reeks, Second Officer Reynolds and the ship's carpenter (from left to right).

away I regarded as entirely providential. The boat was just ordered away, when noticing a rope hanging from the davits I climbed the davit, slid down the rope and dropped into the boat just as she moved off. We had barely time to get fifty yards from the *Stella* when she foundered, and as it appeared to me must have broken in two. As the aft part slipped beneath the water the for'ard part followed, forming an acute angle as each disappeared.

Six boats in all got away, not a bad record as representing twelve minutes' work.

In our boat there were twenty-five of us and as the boat would probably be certified for only eighteen the danger was not yet over. Our experiences until picked up fifteen hours later cannot be described so soon after the happening. The dangers from swamping, from being carried back by the tide and the current to the dangerous Casquet rocks, made the hours of the night full of anxious fear and foreboding. We had in tow the whole time a smaller boat containing ten ladies and a gentleman and a boy, with two sailors to man the oars. A treacherous sea was running the whole time, with thick weather. We toiled all night to keep our boat away from the dreaded Casquets but hardly ever knew our position, until 6.30 a.m. when the fog lifted and we rejoiced to see bearing down in our direction a steamer, which proved to the *Lynx* from Weymouth.

Among those lost on the *Stella* was Captain Reeks, and Mrs Mary Rogers, a stewardess who gave up her lifebelt to a passenger and refused to take her place in one of the boats in orderthatapassengercouldtakeitinhe order that a passenger could take it in her place. In Liverpool Cathedral there can be seen a memorial window dedicated to Mary Rogers, 'A noble woman'.

The high loss of life was probably due to the bulkhead giving way, allowing the sea to rush into the engine room and stake hold, causing the boilers to explode, ripping the steel hull apart: this would have caused the vessel to sink within a very short time.

TSS Channel Queen

The *Channel Queen* was delivered to the Plymouth, Channel Island & Brittany Steamship Co. by her builders, Craggs of Middlesborough, in 1895 to replace the paddle steamer *Aguila*. Under the command of Captain Collings, who had made over two thousand crossings to the Channel Islands, the *Channel Queen* steamed into disaster in the early morning of 1 February 1898. She had left Plymouth the night before at 11 p.m. with fifty passengers and a crew of eighteen. The weather on passage was misty with a heavy swell running, but giving no cause for alarm. On nearing the Hanois lighthouse thick fog was encountered. Captain Colling ordered 'slow ahead' and the lookouts were put on alert, but fate had played her hand and at 5.15 a.m. the ship struck the Black Rock off Portinfer. The impact was so severe that the steamer immediately began to sink. The lifeboats were lowered; one swamped and sank within a few minutes while the rest, after some confusion, managed to pull to the shore a mile and a half away. Ten people lost their lives.

A month later the local newspaper reported, 'The steamer lies in pieces. The funnels lie 30 feet away from the hull, after portions of the ship have been carried farther away. At low tide some of the wreck is visible above the water and piles of wreckage have been washed up along the shores.'

Sarnia

The ketch *Sarnia* was built in Guernsey during 1894 for the French trade, mainly carrying general cargo between St Peter Port and St Malo. She was 79 feet long, with a beam of 18 feet and a draft of 7 feet.

The ship was returning from St Malo on 4 Feburary 1897 with a crew of four and one passenger, John Renier, a Guernsey pilot. While nearing the Ferriere Rocks at 5 a.m. the next morning, *Sarnia* ploughed onto the rocks of Taubarre, which lie northeast of the Ferrieres. All took to her boat and stayed by the stricken vessel for several hours in the hope that at high tide she would free herself, but although she did come off she immediately became stuck on other rocks nearby. As nothing could be done, they rowed to St Peter Port, which they reached safely at 9 a.m. At a later inquiry it was found that the captain was at fault and his certificate was withdrawn.

Sarnia was later salvaged and bought by Bird Bros who owned her until 1903, when she was purchased by W. Stranger who kept her until 1905. In that year she left Guernsey and was taken to the Scilly Isles. On 27 August 1910 she was finally sunk in a collision with a steamer off Lynmouth.

Passengers and officers on the *Ella* taking the sea air. The ship was built in 1881 and served on the L & SWR Co. Channel Islands run for thirty-two years.

However, her sister ship, the *Hilda*, built in 1882, was wrecked off St Malo in November 1905.

SS Alert

The little steamer *Serk*, originally named *Alert*,
disembarking her passengers at Creux Harbour,
Sark at the turn of the century. Apart from
carrying passengers and mails, *Serk* was also
used for towing.

PS Brighton

Brighton, 256 gross tons, was owned by the W & CISP Co. who purchased her from the B & SCR Co. She probably made her first trip to the Islands in 1857, and became a regular visitor until she was wrecked on a voyage from Weymouth to Guernsey on 29 January 1887.

The ship struck the Braye rocks in the Little Russel and sank within a quarter of an hour: all her passengers were saved. During an inquiry it was found that the master had not used the lead to ascertain the depth of water while in poor visibility after passing the Casquets. At the time of the impact *Brighton* was travelling at 11 knots. Her captain's certificate was withdrawn for six months.

Steam Tug Assistance

Assistance, owned by the Garnet Towing Co., arrived in Guernsey in 1886; she had been built by J.M. Arthur & Co. of Paisley. Later she was purchased by the Guernsey Steam Towing Co. The 90 foot vessel 82 tons gross, was used for harbour work and towing and also took trippers to Herm and Sark.

Like her contemporaries, the tug carried out salvage work and was responsible for towing several ships into safe waters. Among them was the ketch *Labrori*, towed in heavy seas; the French schooner *Germaine*, which went ashore in St Sampson's and was pulled off; and the dismasted ketch *Pleiades*, in trouble in the Great Russel – all in 1901.

In 1904 the steamer *Roman*, 750 tons, was towed off from Hanois. She had shipped water in rough weather which reached her cargo, and the carpenter, first mate and steward were overcome by the resulting ammonia fumes, the first two later dying.

While towing the three-masted brigantine *Dunsinane* into St Peter Port in 1904 *Assistance* was struck by SS *Vera*, leaving for Jersey with trippers. The tug was hit on the extreme end of her starboard bow, while in the meantime *Dunsinane* came bow-on to her stern and smashed part of her starboard quarter. The only damage to the brigantine was a broken spar; there was none to the *Vera*.

The tug went to Southampton in 1908 and was later sold there.

SS Fox

On the night of 17 June 1888 the little steamer
Fox was approaching Guernsey from Stockton-
on-Tees carrying 100 tons of water pipes and
100 tons of coal. Unfortunately, contemporary
information is sparse, but it is known that the
Fox, under a Captain Anderson, encountered
thick weather as she neared the Islands: she
struck a rock east of Herm at around 9 p.m. and
later grounded in Belval Bay. Some days later
she was towed off by the tug *Rescue II* and
taken to St Sampson's Harbour.

SS Caesarea

The first *Caesarea* was launched on 7 January
1867 by Aitken & Mansell of Glasgow, for the
L & SWR Co. She was 187 feet long, had 100
berths and could carry up to 350 tons of cargo.
The ship stayed in service on the Channel
Island mail service, and also sailing to St Malo,
for seventeen years until she was wrecked in
1884.

At 2 a.m. on 27 June and in dense fog 10 miles
off Cape de la Hague, *Caesarea* collided with SS
Strathesk, bound from Jersey to Littlehampton
with a cargo of potatoes. The ferry had left
Southampton the previous evening for St Malo
carrying freight; also on board were twelve
French seamen and a lady as passengers. The
vessel was struck amidships and sank within a
very few minutes: all but one survived, a
French seaman being lost and they were
transferred to the *Strathesk*.

PS Tug Rescue

Rescue was constructed for £2,300 by Hepple & Co. of South Shields in 1869 and owned by the Guernsey Steam Towing Co. of St Sampson. From contemporary photographs the paddle tug gives the appearance of being a very pretty little craft, sporting a tall buff funnel, single foremast and a fine clinker-built hull. Apparently she was an excellent sea boat, 85 feet long and 82 tons gross, with plenty of space on board, in fact enough to carry twelve head of cattle. Apart from her normal duties as a tug, her owners would advertise her for excursion trips in the summer.

A contemporary handbill of the day states, 'The *Rescue* will be open for engagements by parties during the summer months at the following low rates: to Jersey £6; if returning within 24 hours £9, not to exceed 100 passengers. To Sark £5, single journey only £3; to Herm £3, single journey only £2, not to exceed 200 passengers. Twenty-four hour notice.' The photo shows her taking trippers to Sark.

Over the years the tug played her part in giving assistance to many ships in distress, including the 1,230 ton screw steamer *Avon* in 1871. En route from Liverpool to Bordeaux with provisions and ammunition, she developed engine trouble and consequently the little tug took her in tow to Guernsey.

The paddle steamer *Aquila* at White Rock, St Peter
Port, c. 1880. She ran regularly to the Islands and was
owned by the W & CISP Co.

SS South Western

The L & SWR Co. steamer *South Western* was built at Blackwall in 1874 as a single-screw steamer of 674 tons gross. Although she was never totally wrecked, she had by no means a quiet life. Her first run to the Channel Islands was in 1875 and she was the first steamer of the company equipped with radio, as an experiment.

In December 1881 she was involved in a collision with a Norwegian barque and in July 1893 was again in collision, with the *Bay Fisher*. In the First World War the *South Western* was torpedoed and sunk by a German submarine.

PS Tug Rescue II

The new *Rescue II* went into service in 1878
under the same owners as the original tug,
which she replaced. She was built by the same
firm and along very similar lines to her predecessor. Her main duties again involved
towing sailing vessels and making occasional
excursions to Sark and Herm.

The photo shows her lying just outside the
tiny harbour at Creux, Sark amid a crowd of
small local boats.

PS Harve

The Platte Boue off Guernsey claimed yet another paddle steamer belonging to the L & SWR Co. when *Harve*, en route from Southampton to Guernsey on 17 February 1875, struck the rock and became a total loss. Her passengers and crew, plus the mails, were saved by being transferred to the L & SWR Co. steamer *Honfleur*. During March 1875 a group of divers working near Burhou decided to change their site and investigated the *Harve*. She was found broken in three and lying slightly across the previously wrecked paddle steamer *Waverley*, which appeared to be in two sections (as she is shown in the painting).

A contemporary illustration depicting the rescue of passengers from the *Harve*.

PS Waverley

The *Waverley* was originally owned by the NBSP Co. and was purchased by the L & SWR Co. in 1868, arriving in Guernsey in December. She was a fine twin-funnelled paddler, 592 tons gross, and 222 feet long with a low freeboard and no forecastle head; in fact she had been designed as a blockade runner for the American Civil War and was built by A. & J. Inglis in 1865. Her career was short-lived, for she was wrecked on 5 June 1873 on the Platte Boue. There was no loss of life and the mails for the island were saved. Within two days of striking the ship broke up and her remains were bought by W. W. Bird for scrap. However, the salvage company apparently managed to lift only six davits and two ladders from the wreck.

Louisa

The barque *Louisa* was sighted on 16 January 1872 in distress NW of Guernsey and a large number of craft put to sea from St Sampson's and other harbours along the coast. On reaching the stricken ship they found her apparently abandoned by her crew. The hulk was at once taken in tow by the paddle steamer *Rescue* and berthed in St Peter Port. She was eventually towed to the mainland and sold back to her builders.

It was later discovered that the London registered barque, 905 tons gross and built in 1860, had left Quebec on 16 November for an English port. At 2 p.m. on 8 December when 50 miles SSW of the lizard she encountered heavy seas, and at 6 p.m. was struck broadside by a tremendous wave. Within less than a quarter of an hour she turned upside down and her crew of seventeen were struggling for their lives in the raging winter sea. Four men were swept away and drowned but the remainder managed to climb onto her keel. After three hours *Louisa*'s masts carried away and she began to right herself; fortunately her crew managed to scramble onto the deck. On board they found boats and spars washed away, the accommodation gutted and fresh water contaminated. During the next day several vessels were sighted but none made any attempt to render assistance and it was not until several days later that the crew was picked up by a Swedish brig.

PS Normandy

The iron paddle steamer *Normandy*, built for the L & S W R Co. by J. Ash & Co. of London, first arrived at Jersey on 19 September 1863, under Captain Babot. From contemporary reports she was a graceful craft with good sea-going qualities, 600 tons gross, and 210 feet long. Captain Babot was quoted as saying that the responsibility of having the *Normandy* under his command would add ten years to his life. She was the first Channel Island steamer to have a straight stem: I would have preferred to see her with a more graceful flared bow.

Normandy served on the Channel Islands run for seven years until she was run down by the SS *Mary* on 17 March 1870 with the loss of thirty-three lives. The collision occurred in dense fog, 20 to 25 miles southwest of the Needles. A contemporary account of the disaster follows.

When the *Mary* was first sighted by the *Normandy* it is said the former had no masthead light up, her red sidelight only being seen, but this is accounted for by the statement that the lamp had at that moment been taken down for the purpose of being

The *Normandy* lying in front of various other ships. Her two steeply raked masts only carried sail for auxiliary propulsion and to steady her motion; they hardly compare in effectiveness with the much taller mast behind her, although they were well matched to the packet's overall appearance.

trimmed. The circumstances, however, somewhat misled the chief officer of the *Normandy* who fancied that the *Mary* was a sailing vessel. Her masthead light not being up, the *Normandy* did not sight her as soon as would otherwise have been the case, and which might, humanely speaking, have prevented the accident and its terrible consequences. That the *Normandy* still continued at her usual rate of speed is explained by the fact that up to that time of the occurrence she had experienced clear weather. The mate only a minute before sighting the *Mary* discovered the fog, and observing which he sent for the captain, who was then in his cabin. Captain Harvey came on deck immediately, but he had no sooner reached it than the *Mary* was observed. He also then heard the mate ask the man at the wheel if the helm was hard-a-starboard, to which he replied 'Yes sir' and the captain rejoined, 'Keep it so', and likewise ordered him to standby the engines to stop the ship if necessary. Captain Harvey looked over the side of the vessel and seeing the position of the approaching steamer directed the helmsman to put the helm hard over and to keep it so while he himself hastened to the bridge. No sooner was this done, than the collision occurred.

The course adopted by the captain of the *Mary* is highly commendable. On hearing Captain Harvey call to him for boats he did his duty nobly. Out of his six seamen, he sent four with a second mate to the relief of the passengers, and he was under the impression that they were pulling hard for the *Normandy*, for which he had given explicit instructions, telling his men also that the ship was going

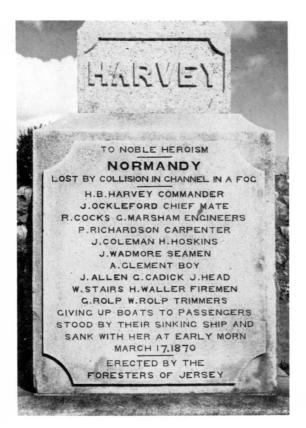

TO NOBLE HEROISM
NORMANDY
LOST BY COLLISION IN CHANNEL IN A FOG
H.B.HARVEY COMMANDER
J.OCKLEFORD CHIEF MATE
R.COCKS G.MARSHAM ENGINEERS
P.RICHARDSON CARPENTER
J.COLEMAN H.HOSKINS
J.WADMORE SEAMEN
A.CLEMENT BOY
J.ALLEN G.CADICK J.HEAD
W.STAIRS H.WALLER FIREMEN
G.ROLP W.ROLP TRIMMERS
GIVING UP BOATS TO PASSENGERS
STOOD BY THEIR SINKING SHIP AND
SANK WITH HER AT EARLY MORN
MARCH 17.1870
ERECTED BY THE
FORESTERS OF JERSEY

down. The *Normandy*'s boats, however, passed this boat, and it is reported that one of the men in her was heard to say that as the *Normandy* was going down the boat would be filled and they would all be swamped. From some cause or other which remains to be explained, the boat returned to the *Mary* and the second mate, we are informed, asked the captain whether he was to go on, to which he replied 'What did I put you in the boat for but to go on?' To this one circumstance attributed a greater sacrifice of life than would otherwise have been the case. The lifeboat from the *Mary* would have held all, or nearly all, those left on board the *Normandy* who might presumably have been saved by that means. What added to the misfortune also was that the steamers lost sight of each other in the fog. The *Normandy*'s whistle was kept blowing, and the second mate of the vessel states that he heard it till he got close alongside the *Mary* and it ceased, and at that time the *Normandy* is supposed to have foundered.

A gentleman who was on board at the time the collision took place heard the whistle blow and about two or three minutes afterwards a tremendous crash took place, accompanied by a great rush of water through the ladies' cabin and the lavatory. All the ladies were called up and got on deck as soon as possible, the boats being manned and made ready for lowering. They were then lowered by the captain's orders and all the ladies that could be found, put in them. About 10 or 15 minutes after the collision the water was making over the taffrail and the saloon deck was springing up by the force of the water underneath. At the time the boats were lowered the swell was so great that it was with great difficulty that they could be prevented from being stove in.

When the boats returned no one could be seen in the water, a somewhat remarkable fact especially when it is considered that there was a ladder on the deck which would have held up perhaps a dozen people, besides other large articles, but the true explanation is probably found in the strength of the eddying created when the ship went down. Various things were found floating about, among them one of the deck cushions, some stocks of rockets, etc. The boat crew reported that they heard a terrible shriek when about halfway between the two ships. Some of the ladies in the *Normandy* came on deck to get into the boats in a deplorable condition, three of them having nothing but their nightdresses on. One lady lost some valuable jewellery and about fifty sovereigns. A passenger threw a case belonging to him into the boat, but he did not get in himself and was drowned. Some of the passengers, however, saved their carpetbags. With regard to the four female passengers who were in the forepart of the *Normandy* it is necessary to explain why they were not saved. It was the strict order and desire of Captain Harvey that they should get into the boat and they were repeatedly urged to do so, in fact one of the male passengers was heard to shout to them 'Do as you were desired!' At that time there was no water at the end of the vessel where the ladies stood and they seem to have yielded to the persuasion of the naval seaman, who told them that he was going to stay where he was, and they had better do the same as there would be more chance of getting into a boat. This statement coupled with the appearance of water breaking over the quarterdeck most probably induced these unfortunate passengers to remain on board, either in the expectation that the *Normandy* would still float, or that there would be other boats coming in which there would be more room for them.

Among those lost on the *Normandy* was her master, Captain Harvey. A later inquiry found that he was to blame for the tragic accident: apparently the *Normandy* should have given way as the *Mary* was in fog at the time. However, it is also fair to say that while Captain Harvey was in charge of the ship at the time of the accident, the officer on the bridge should have slowed his engines when he approached the fog, which he did not.

PS Dispatch

The paddle steamer *Dispatch*, 265 tons gross, first arrived in Jersey early in May 1848. Her main run was between Southampton and Le Havre or Guernsey. During a particularly violent storm in October 1853, HMSS *Dasher* came to her assistance when in distress off Corbiere, Jersey. *Dasher*, a 250 ton paddle steamer, had begun carrying mail between Weymouth and the Islands in 1838. She stayed only a comparatively short time in service and in 1848 was withdrawn to take up new duties as a survey vessel.

An interesting account was given in the *London Illustrated News* on 29 October 1853:

Perilous Situation of the Steam Packet *Dispatch* at Guernsey

The mail steam packet *Dispatch*, Captain Babot, left the harbour of St Helier at her usual hour on Monday the 17th inst. for Guernsey and Southampton, in a heavy gale and high sea. Soon after nine o'clock she was signalled at Fort Regent as in distress; and the following are the particulars of the accident which had befallen her.

When she arrived off Corbière her main shaft broke in two places and two eccentric rods also snapped, at once rendering her steam machinery unusable for further navigation. In this extremity Captain Babot attempted to make sail to return, but in setting the mainsail the peak halyard block broke, and when it was replaced the halyard broke. He then let go anchors between the three rocks called the Oaks. HM steamship *Dasher*, Cdr Lefebvre, on perceiving the distress signal had immediately left the harbour to go to her assistance; and when the *Dispatch* saw her approaching within about 1½ miles she cut her cable leaving the anchor and about 30 fathom of line, and got under way.

The *Dasher* met her near Corbière and going round her stern observed that she was drifting to leeward; she then took her in tow with two hawsers. These broke short one after another and were again

Dasher towing the Jersey mail packet *Dispatch* off Corbiere, both ships helped by the following wind. Engraving from a sketch by R. J. Ouless of Jersey.

replaced in the same manner. The wind being fair, the *Dasher* relied mainly on her canvas, working her engines now and then to keep the vessels clear of each other. The *Dasher* encountered some tremendous seas; one of them went high over her bridge, and carried away the stern-boat from the davits, leaving the deck so encumbered with water as to render it necessary to knock out the ports for its escape. Shortly after twelve o'clock she arrived safely with her rescued companion in the outer roads of St Helier, and at twenty minutes to four o'clock, the anxious crowds assembled on the pierheads had the delight of seeing the war steamer passing safely in Victoria Harbour, tugging after her the disabled *Dispatch*. As the *Dasher* passed between the pierheads, several hearty cheers greeted her gallant Commander and crew, from the assembled throngs on the pier and the quay.

We need scarcely state that the alarm among the packet's passengers (among whom was a lady with nine children, one only six weeks old) when they found her disabled and at the mercy of the wind and tide, on such a terrible coast, was extreme. Many of them knelt and prayed.

One of the passengers in the *Dispatch* has since addressed a letter to the paper complaining of the want of attention of the authorities. He says:

I was one of the passengers on board the *Dispatch* steam packet ... when she so narrowly escaped shipwreck on the Jersey coast; and I think it is my duty to suggest that a full investigation into the disaster should be made by the Post Office or some other competent authority, and a report be published. Why should there not be an inquiry when upwards of one hundred lives were placed in such terrible peril? The first cause of the accident was the breaking of the main intermediate shaft, which carried away the eccentrics. This main shaft appeared to have been rusted on one side, at the fracture, to the extent of nearly half its diameter, and must have sustained great injury before. Orders were given to hoist the mainsail, but the iron halyard block broke and the steamer became perfectly powerless. In this perilous position it was of the utmost importance that the immediate intelligence of our danger should be conveyed to St Helier. About eight o'clock a distress signal was made on the steamer. After rather a long delay, a gun was fired and repeated twice. It must have been full an hour before the signal was answered at the signal station; and I have since learned that it did not reach St Helier's till half past nine, and in the form of 'for steamers' (which was unintelligible) instead of 'steamer in distress', to which it was afterwards changed. I think I have shown ample reason for an inquiry into the state of the machinery and sailing tackle of the ship, and into the signal service at Jersey. No one can more admire than I do the gallantry of Captain Lefebvre and the crew of HM steamship *Dasher*, and those who voluntarily accompanied him; and I feel deeply grateful to the Almighty, and under him to those brave men, for the timely succour afforded at such a hazard; also to the brave crew of the Jersey pilot boat, who courageously came off to render assistance but met us in tow of the *Dasher*.

Dispatch stayed in service until 1885 when she was converted into a coal hulk and in the early 1890s she was broken up.

PS Express

Express was one of three sister ships built for the South Western Steam Packet Co. by Ditchburn & Mare; the others being *Courier* and *Dispatch*. The three vessels were built on similar lines and could attain 15 knots, which for their size was a fine achievement. Sadly the *Express*, used on the Southampton to Le Harve or the Channel Islands routes, did not fare as well as her sisters.

Courier served until 1875 and *Dispatch* until 1885, while *Express* came to grief on Les Boiteaux, a group of rocks off Corbiere, Jersey, on 20 September 1859. The impact on the rocks made a large tear in the port bow of the vessel, allowing the sea to rush in with tremendous force. Fortunately for those on board, the ship managed to limp into St Brelade Bay, were she went grounded and became a total wreck.

Apart from two passengers who died from drowning when they panicked and jumped overboard, all were saved. Also on board were three race horses being shipped to Guernsey for a local race meeting. They were rescued by placing bedding on the rocks leading to the shore, giving a firm foothold to the ground beyond.

The wrecked *Express* in St Brelade Bay, 1859. The lithograph was executed by C. Chabot and published by Gosset & Co. The artist is unknown, but the original may well have been painted by P. J. Ouless, who lived in Jersey.

PS Superb

The Jersey Steam Packet Co. paddle steamer *Superb*, 136 feet long, had been built in 1839 by Napiers in Glasgow and ran between the Islands and also to St Malo and Granville. She was wrecked with fifty passengers on board when bound from St Malo to Jersey on 24 September 1850, after hitting the Minquiers at full speed. Seventeen lives were lost during the disaster; eleven were drowned when they panicked in their lifeboat and it capsized: it is not recorded how the remaining passengers perished. Those left on board managed to climb onto the rocks and were rescued safely. *Superb*'s master, Captain Priaulx, was involved in a sixteen-year court battle as to his conduct of the whole affair, but it was never resolved as he died at the age of seventy-two before the case could be concluded. The ship became a total wreck, though her boiler was recovered and refitted into the paddle steamer *Rose* built by F.C. Clarke of Jersey.

A contemporary painting depicting the *Superb* hitting the Minquiers.

PS Queen of the Isles

Following her launch in 1853, from the Newcastle yard of Thomas Toward, the *Queen of the Isles* was employed on the inter-island service carrying passengers, cargo and live-stock; she also ran excursions to France and elsewhere. Her appearance must have been most regal with a full-length figurehead of Queen Victoria and a lion rampant on either side, surmounted by the vessel's name, plus a liberal amount of carved woodwork and moulding. Below she had a saloon furnished with velvet cushions, and berths for passengers. Her seagoing qualities, however, were somewhat less impressive: she frequently leaked, much to the terror of her passengers. Indeed it is remarkable that she did not join the list of wrecked ships in Channel Island waters, as her design was in keeping for river work than the sea. With a draft of 10 feet, she was

Queen of the Isles in St Peter Port, circa 1865. The figurehead of Queen Victoria can be seen on her bow.

100 feet long and only 17 feet wide.

A delightfully graphic account written by an unwary passenger who travelled in the ship from Cherbourg to Alderney in 1854, clearly shows the difficulties her officers and crew had in coping with the little paddler while she was underway at sea.

On this occasion the vessel had about a hundred persons on board, and in addition six or eight oxen and a considerable number of sheep on deck. This top weight, added to her defective constitution, caused her when on passage, although the weather was moderate, to list over so alarmingly as to make those on board – particularly mature men – apprehend that she was about to capsize. She remained in this perilous position for some time to the terror of all on board, and she was only righted by all the passengers being sent to the upper side of the deck. We are assured by competent persons who were on board that the vessel was in extreme danger and that, hampered as she was with top weight, had it been necessary suddenly to give her much helm, she would have been thrown on her beam ends and gone down with all on board. The courage and seamanship of Captain Scott, which are so well known, would have availed nothing and a frightful catastrophe would have happened.

In 1857 *Queen of the Isles* had a major overhaul and refit which made her considerably better able to tackle the dangerous waters of the Islands. In July 1870 she struck a flat rock in dense fog two miles northeast of Alderney. Amid great panic two of her boats were launched, causing even more commotion as the passengers then made a headlong rush to secure places in them. Eventually order was restored with the ladies being put into the boats and taken to a nearby rock where they were landed safely and the rest of the passengers followed.

On the high tide the paddle steamer floated clear of the rock and went into deep water. Finding that she was not leaking, the captain made preparations to take his passengers on board again and make headway. All but twenty-five returned to the ship, they deciding that it was safer on the rock. The captain, finding that his assurances were of no avail, gave them blankets and provisions to fortify them through the night. By early morning, their desire to be castaways had waned and they returned to the ship, which then proceeded safely to Alderney.

The *Queen of the Isles* was taken out of service in 1872.

Bibliography

PHILIP ASHIER, *Stories of Jersey Seas, of Jersey Coast and Jersey Seamen* Part Two. The Advertiser Press, Huddersfield

BOB BAKER, *Stranded Juggernaut*. Guernsey Lithoprint, Guernsey 1974.

VICTOR COYSH, *Island Steam Packets*. La Sociètè Guernsiaise, Guille-Allès Library, Guernsey 1977

CHARLES CRUICKSHANK, *The German Occupation of the Channel Islands*. Published for the Trustees of the Imperial War Museum by the Guernsey Press, 1975

J.M. DAVID, *Wrecks in the Bailwick with Corrections and Additional Details by Eric W. Sharp*. Sociètè Guernsiaise, 1961–7.

JACK DIAMOND, editor, *Prosperity & Merchant Navy Memorial*, 1975. Published to commemorate the unveiling of a memorial to those who lost their lives in the MV *Prosperity*

C.L.D. DUCKWORTH and G.E. LANGMUIR, *Railway and Other Steamers*. Shipping Histories, 1948

BRIAN J. DUQUEMIN, *The Bailiwick of Guernsey: the Jubilee Years 1952–1977*. Cobo, Guernsey 1977

PETER KEMP, *Oxford Companion to Ships and the Sea*. Granada Publishing, 1979.

Lloyd's Register of Shipping

London Illustrated News, 1850

A.H.S. LUCAS, *An Alderney Scrap-Book*. The Alderney Society, 1972

L.H. LUCKING, *The Great Western at Weymouth*. David & Charles, 1971

RALPH MOLLET, *A Chronology of Jersey*. Sociètè Jersiaise, 1954

J.E. MOULLIN, *Guernsey Ways*. The Guernsey Press

Index of Ships

Alert 106

Aquila 112–13

Armas 37

Arnold Maersk 46

Assistance 108

Beauport 50–1

Big Apple 22–4

Brighton 107

Brockley Coombe 41

Burton 65

Caesarea 110

Caesarea II 58–9

Captain Niko 38

Channel Queen 103

Charles Ellison 65

Constantia S 39

Courier II 80–2

HMS *Dasher* 121–2

Dispatch 121–2

Dunsinane 90–1

Ella 105

Elwood Mead 34–6

Emily Eveson 61

Express 123

Felix de Abasolo 69

Fermain 42

Fox 109

Franz Westermann 44–5

Groningen 19

Harve 116

Helma 45

Henny Frickle 47

Hilda 2, 86–9

Ibex 96–8

International 76

Iris 55

Isle of Jersey 52–3

Jenne 62

La Salle 39

Leros 77

Linn O'Dee 72

Liverpool 92–3

Lorina 52–3

Louisa 118

Maina 70

Mary Anne 63

Nordgnskjold 73

Normandy 119–20

Oil-rig barge 25

Oost Vlaanderen 43

Orion 18–21

Overton 48–9

Pegase 28–9

Petit Raymond 84

Point Law 26–7

President Garcia 38

Princess Ena 56–7

Prosperity 30–3

Queen of the Isles 125–6

Rap 71

Rescue 111

Rescue II 115

Rhenania 64

Ribbledale 30

Roebuck 66–8, 95

Sarnia 104

Serk 106

South Western 114

Stella 99–102

Superb 124

Swansea 78–9

Tomi 22

Tommeliten 48

Trignac 85

HMS *Viper* 83

Waverley 117